Lectionary
Advent 2019 to the eve of Advent 2020 (Year A)

Church House Publishing

Published by	Church House Publishing Church House Great Smith Street London SW1P 3AZ
Compilation ©	*The Archbishops' Council 2019*
ISBN	978-0-7151-2355-3 (standard) 978-0-7151-2356-0 (large)

Copyright and Acknowledgements	*The Revised Common Lectionary* is copyright © The Consultation on Common Texts: 1992. The Church of England adaptations to the Principal Service Lectionary are copyright © The Archbishops' Council, as are the Second and Third Service Lectionaries, the Weekday Lectionary for Morning and Evening Prayer and the Additional Weekday Lectionary.

The Daily Eucharistic Lectionary derives, with some adaptation, from the *Ordo Lectionum Missae* of the Roman Catholic Church and is reproduced by permission of The International Commission on English in the Liturgy.

Edited by Peter Moger
Designed by Derek Birdsall & John Morgan/Omnific
Typeset by RefineCatch Ltd, Bungay, Suffolk
Printed in England by Core Publications Ltd

Contents of this booklet

This booklet gives details of the full range of possibilities envisaged in the liturgical calendar and lectionary of Common Worship. Its use as a tool for the preparation of worship will require the making of several choices based first on the general celebration of the Christian year by the Church of England as a whole; second on the customary pattern of calendar in the diocese, parish and place of worship; and third on the pattern of services locally.

The **first column** comprises the Calendar of the Church with the days of the year. Observances that are mandatory are printed either in **bold** type (Sundays), in **bold** type (Principal Feasts and Holy Days) or in roman (Festivals). Optional celebrations (Lesser Festivals) and Commemorations are printed in ordinary roman type and *italic* type respectively.

The **second column** comprises (a) the readings and psalms for the Principal Service on Sundays, Principal Feasts and Holy Days, and Festivals, and (b) Holy Communion readings and psalms for other days of the week. On the Sundays after Trinity, the Old Testament reading and its psalm are divided into two smaller columns, indicating a choice between a 'continuous' reading week by week or a reading 'related' to the Gospel for that day.

The **third column** comprises (a) the Third Service readings and psalms for Sundays, Principal Feasts and Holy Days and Festivals, and (b) the readings and psalms for weekday Morning Prayer.

The **fourth column** comprises (a) the Second Service readings and psalms for Sundays, Principal Feasts and Holy Days and Festivals, and (b) the readings and psalms for weekday Evening Prayer.

An **Additional Weekday Lectionary**, intended particularly for use in places of worship that attract occasional rather than daily worshippers, is provided on pages 69–76. It may be used either at Morning or Evening Prayer.

Common of the Saints

General readings and psalms for saints' days can be found on pages 79–83; for some particular celebrations, other readings are suggested there.

Special Occasions

Readings and psalms for special occasions can be found on pages 84–85.

Liturgical colours

Appropriate liturgical colours are suggested in this booklet. They are not mandatory; traditional or local use may be followed.

Colours are indicated by single letters: the first (always upper case) for the season or Festival; and occasionally a second (lower case) for an optional celebration on that day. Thus, for example, Gr for the celebration of a Lesser Festival whose liturgical colour is red, in an otherwise 'green' season.

The following abbreviations are used:

G	Green
P or p	Purple or Violet
P(La)	Purple or Lent array
R or r	Red
W or w	White (Gold is indicated where its use would be appropriate)

—

Notes on the Lectionary

Sundays, Principal Feasts and Holy Days and Festivals

Three sets of psalms and readings are provided for each Sunday, Principal Feast or Holy Day and Festival.

The **Principal Service lectionary** (based on the Revised Common Lectionary) is intended for use at the principal service of the day (whether this service is Holy Communion or some other authorized form). In most Church communities, this is likely to be the mid-morning service, but the minister is free to decide which service time normally constitutes the Principal Service of the day. This lectionary may be used twice if required – for example, at an early celebration of Holy Communion and then again at a later one.

If only **two readings** are used at the Principal Service and that service is Holy Communion, the second reading must always be the Gospel reading. When the Principal Service lectionary is used at a service other than Holy Communion, the Gospel reading need not always be chosen.

The **Second Service lectionary** is intended for a second main service. In many churches, this lectionary may be the appropriate provision for a Sunday afternoon or evening service. A Gospel reading is always provided so that this lectionary can, if necessary, be used where the second main service is a celebration of Holy Communion.

The **Third Service lectionary**, with shorter readings, is intended where a third set of psalms and readings is needed and is most appropriate for use at an office. A Gospel reading is not always provided, so this lectionary is not suitable for use at Holy Communion.

Weekdays

The Common Worship Weekday Lectionary authorized by the General Synod in 2005 comprises a lectionary (with psalms) for Holy Communion, a lectionary for Morning and Evening Prayer and tables of psalms for Morning and Evening Prayer.

The **Daily Eucharistic Lectionary** (based on the Roman Catholic daily eucharistic lectionary) is a semi-continuous two-year lectionary with a wide use of scripture, though not complete coverage of the Bible. Two readings are provided for each day, the first from either the Old or New Testament, the second always a Gospel. Psalm provision is intended to be a brief response to the first reading. It is for use at Holy Communion normally in places with a daily or near-daily celebration with a regular congregation. It may also be used as an office lectionary.

The **lectionary for Morning and Evening Prayer** always provides two readings for each office, the first from the Old Testament and the second from the New Testament. These are generally in sequence. One of the New Testament readings for any particular day is from the Gospels.

The **psalms for Morning and Evening Prayer** follow a sequential pattern in Ordinary Time (apart from the period from All Saints to the beginning of Advent).

In the periods from All Saints until 18 December, from the Epiphany until the Presentation of Christ in the Temple (Candlemas), from Ash Wednesday until Palm Sunday, and from the Monday after Easter Week until Pentecost, there is a choice of psalms at Morning and Evening Prayer. The psalms printed first reflect the theme of the season. Alternatively, the psalms from the Ordinary Time cycle may be used. The two sets are separated by 'or'.

From 19 December until the Epiphany and from the Monday of Holy Week until the Saturday of Easter Week, only seasonal psalms are provided.

Where more than one psalm is given, one psalm (printed in **bold**) may be used as the sole psalm at that office.

Guidance on how these options for saying the psalms are expressed typographically can be found in the 'Notes on the Lectionary' below.

A further cycle is provided (see table on page 86), which is largely the monthly sequential cycle of psalms given in the *Book of Common Prayer*.

A single psalm for use by those who only say one office each day is provided in Prayer During the Day in *Common Worship: Daily Prayer*.

An **Additional Weekday Lectionary**, intended particularly for use in places of worship that attract occasional rather than daily worshippers, is provided on pages 69–76. It can be used either at Morning or Evening Prayer. Psalmody is not provided and should be taken from the provision outlined above.

Using the Lectionary tables

All **Bible references** (except to the Psalms) are to the *New Revised Standard Version* (New York, 1989). Those who use other Bible translations should check the verse numbers against the *NRSV*. Each reference gives book, chapter and verse, in that order.

References to the Psalms are to the Common Worship psalter, published in Common Worship: Services and Prayers for the Church of England (2000) and Common Worship: Daily Prayer (2005). A table showing the verse number differences between this and the psalter in the Book of Common Prayer is provided on the Common Worship website (https://www.churchofengland.org/prayer-and-worship/worship-texts-and-resources/common-worship/daily-prayer/psalter/psalter-verse).

Options in the provision of readings or psalms are presented in the following ways:

¶ square brackets [xx] give either optional additional verses or Psalms, or a shorter alternative;

¶ 'or' indicates a simple choice between two alternative readings or courses of psalms;

¶ a psalm printed in **bold** may be used as the sole psalm at that office;

¶ on weekdays a psalm printed in parentheses (xx) is omitted if it has been used as the opening canticle at that office;

¶ a psalm marked with an asterisk may be shortened if desired.

Where a reading from the **Apocrypha** is offered, an alternative Old Testament reading is provided.

In the choice of **readings other than the Gospel** reading, the minister should ensure that, in any year, a balance is maintained between readings from the Old and New Testaments and that, where a particular biblical book is appointed to be read over several weeks, the choice ensures that the continuity of one book is not lost.

On the Sundays after Trinity, the Principal Service Lectionary provides **alternative Old Testament readings and psalms**. References in the left-hand column (under the heading 'Continuous') offer a *semi-continuous* reading of Old Testament texts. Such a reading and its complementary psalmody stand independently of the other readings. References in the right-hand column (under the heading 'Related') *relate* the Old Testament reading and the psalm to the Gospel reading. One column should be followed for the whole sequence of Sundays after Trinity.

The Lectionary 2019–2020

The Sunday and festal readings for 1 December 2019 (the First Sunday of Advent) to 28 November 2020 (the eve of Advent Sunday) are from **Year A**, which offers a semi-continuous reading of Matthew's Gospel at the Principal Service on Sundays throughout the year.

The weekday readings for Holy Communion are from **Year Two** of the Daily Eucharistic Lectionary (DEL).

Office readings are from Table 1 of the Weekday Lectionary at Morning Prayer and from Table 2 of the Weekday Lectionary at Evening Prayer: Old Testament 2a in Seasonal Time and 2b in Ordinary Time, and New Testament 2.

Notes on the Calendar
1 December 2019 —
28 November 2020

These notes are based on the Rules to Order the Christian Year (*Common Worship: Times and Seasons*, pages 24–30).

Sundays

All Sundays celebrate the paschal mystery of the death and resurrection of the Lord. They also reflect the character of the seasons in which they are set.

Principal Feasts

On these days (printed in bold) Holy Communion is celebrated in every cathedral and parish church, and this celebration, required by Canon B 14, may not be displaced by any other celebration, and may be dispensed with only in accordance with the provision of Canon B 14A.

Except in the case of Christmas Day and Easter Day, the celebration of the Feast *begins with Evening Prayer on the day before the Feast*, and the Collect at that Evening Prayer is that of the Feast. In the case of Christmas Eve and Easter Eve, there is proper liturgical provision (including a Collect) for the whole day.

The Epiphany may, for pastoral reasons, be celebrated on Sunday 5 January.

Other Principal Holy Days

These days (printed in bold), and the liturgical provision for them, may not be displaced by any other celebration.

Ash Wednesday (26 February) and **Maundy Thursday** (9 April) are Principal Holy Days. On both these days Holy Communion is celebrated in every cathedral or parish church, except where there is dispensation under Canon B 14A.

Good Friday (10 April) is a Principal Holy Day.

Eastertide

The paschal character of **the Great Fifty Days of Easter**, from Easter Day (12 April) to Pentecost (31 May), should be celebrated throughout the season, and should not be displaced by other celebrations. No Festival day may be celebrated in Easter Week; and nor may any Festival – except for a Patronal or Dedication Festival – displace the celebration of a Sunday (a memorial of the resurrection) during Eastertide. The paschal character of the season should be retained on those weekdays when saints' days are celebrated.

The three days before Ascension Day (18–20 May) are customarily observed as **Rogation Days**, when prayer is offered for God's blessing on the fruits of the earth and on human labour.

The nine days **after Ascension Day until the eve of Pentecost** (22–30 May) are observed as days of prayer and preparation for the celebration of the outpouring of the Holy Spirit.

Ordinary Time

Ordinary Time comprises two periods in the year: first, the period from the day after the Presentation of Christ in the Temple until the day before Ash Wednesday, and second, that from the day after Pentecost until the day before the First Sunday of Advent.

During Ordinary Time, there is no seasonal emphasis, except that the period between All Saints' Day and the First Sunday of Advent is a time to celebrate and reflect upon the reign of Christ in earth and heaven.

Festivals

These days (printed in roman), and the liturgical provision for them, are not usually displaced. For each day there is full liturgical provision for a Principal, Second and Third Service and an optional so-called First Evening Prayer on the evening before the Festival where this is required.

Festivals may not be celebrated on Sundays in Advent, Lent or Eastertide, the Baptism of Christ, Ascension Day, Trinity Sunday or Christ the King, or weekdays between Palm Sunday and the Second Sunday of Easter.

Otherwise, a Festival falling on a Sunday – namely in 2019–20, Luke the Evangelist (falling on the Nineteenth Sunday after Trinity) – may be kept on that Sunday or transferred to the Monday (or, at the discretion of the minister, to the next suitable weekday).

Certain Festivals (namely, Thomas the Apostle, Matthias the Apostle, the Visit of the Blessed Virgin Mary to Elizabeth and the Blessed Virgin Mary) have customary alternative dates (see page 8).

The Thursday after Trinity Sunday (11 June) may be observed as the **Day of Thanksgiving for the Institution of Holy Communion** (sometimes known as Corpus Christi), and may be kept as a Festival; if it is kept as a Festival, St Barnabas the Apostle is transferred to 12 June.

Other Celebrations

Mothering Sunday falls on the Fourth Sunday of Lent (22 March). Alternative prayers and readings are provided for the Principal Service. **Bible Sunday** may be celebrated on 25 October, replacing the Last Sunday after Trinity, and appropriate prayers and readings are provided.

Local Celebrations

The celebration of **the patron saint or the title of a church** is kept either as a Festival or as a Principal Feast.

The **Dedication Festival** of a church is the anniversary of the date of its dedication or consecration. This is kept either as a Festival or as a Principal Feast. When kept as Principal Feasts, the Patronal and Dedication Festivals may be transferred to the nearest Sunday, unless that day is already a Principal Feast or one of the following days: the First Sunday of Advent, the Baptism of Christ, the First Sunday of Lent, the Fifth Sunday of Lent, or Palm Sunday. If the actual date is not known, the Dedication Festival may be celebrated on 4 October (replacing the Seventeenth Sunday after Trinity), or on 25 October (replacing the Last Sunday after Trinity), or on a suitable date chosen locally. Readings can be found on page 77.

Harvest Thanksgiving may be celebrated on any Sunday in autumn, replacing the provision for that day, provided it does not displace any Principal Feast or Festival.

Diocesan and other local provision may be made in **the calendar of the saints** to supplement the general calendar, in accordance with Canon B 6, paragraph 5.

Lesser Festivals

Lesser Festivals (printed in ordinary roman type, in black) are observed in a manner appropriate to a particular place. Each is provided with a Collect, which may supersede the Collect of the week. or certain Lesser Festivals a complete set of Eucharistic readings is provided, and for others appropriate readings may be selected from the Common of the Saints (see pages 79–83). These readings may, at the minister's discretion, supersede the Daily Eucharistic Lectionary (DEL). The weekday psalms and readings at Morning and Evening Prayer are not usually superseded by those for Lesser Festivals, but at the minister's discretion psalms and readings provided on these days for use at Holy Communion may be used instead at Morning or Evening Prayer.

The minister may be selective in the Lesser Festivals that are observed and may also keep some, or all of them, as Commemorations, perhaps especially in Advent, Lent and Easter where the character of the season ought to be sustained. If the Day of Thanksgiving for the Institution of Holy Communion (11 June) is not kept as a Festival in 2020, it is not observed that year, and 11 June is kept as the Festival of Barnabas the Apostle.

When a Lesser Festival falls on a Principal Feast or Holy Day, a Festival, a Sunday, or on a weekday between Palm Sunday and the Second Sunday of Easter, its celebration is normally omitted for that year. However, where there is sufficient reason, it may, at the discretion of the minister, be celebrated on the nearest available day.

Commemorations

Commemorations (printed in *italic*) are made by a mention in prayers of intercession. They are not provided with Collect, Psalm and Readings, and do not replace the usual weekday provision at Holy Communion or at Morning and Evening Prayer.

The minister may be selective in the Commemorations that are made.

Only where there is an established celebration in the wider Church or where the day has a special local significance may a Commemoration be observed as a Lesser Festival, with liturgical provision from the Common of the Saints (pages 79–83).

In designating a Commemoration as a Lesser Festival, the minister must remember the need to maintain the spirit of the season, especially of Advent, Lent and Easter.

Days of Discipline and Self-Denial

The weekdays of Lent and every Friday in the year are days of discipline and self-denial, with the exception of Principal Feasts, Festivals outside Lent, and Fridays from Easter Day to Pentecost. The day preceding a Principal Feast may also be appropriately kept as a day of discipline and self-denial in preparation for the Feast.

Ember Days

Ember Days should be kept, under the bishop's directions, in the week before an ordination as days of prayer for those to be ordained deacon or priest.

Ember Days may also be kept even when there is no ordination in the diocese as more general days of prayer for those who serve the Church in its various ministries, both ordained and lay, and for vocations. Traditionally they have been observed on the Wednesday, Friday and Saturday in the week before the Third Sunday of Advent, the Second Sunday of Lent and the Sundays nearest to 29 June and 29 September.

Notes on Collects

For a table showing where the Collects and Post Communions are published, see page 77.

Where a Collect ends 'through Jesus Christ ... now and for ever', the minister may omit the longer (trinitarian) ending and use the shorter ending, 'through Jesus Christ our Lord', to which the people respond, 'Amen'. The longer ending, however, is to be preferred at a service of Holy Communion.

The Collect for each Sunday is used at Evening Prayer on the Saturday preceding, except where that Saturday is a Principal Feast, or a Festival or the eve of Christmas Day or Easter Day. The Collect for each Sunday is also used on the weekdays following, except where other provision is made.

Abbreviations used in this book

Alt	Alternative	P or p	Purple or Violet
Bp	Bishop	P(La)	Purple or Lent Array
BVM	Blessed Virgin Mary	Ps & Pss	Psalmody
DEL	Daily Eucharistic Lectionary	R or r	Red
EP	Evening Prayer	W or w	White (Gold is indicated where
G	Green		its use would be appropriate)

HC	Holy Communion: used where additional references are given to provide alternative texts for use at a celebration of Holy Communion (most often the provision of a psalm or gospel)
MP	Morning Prayer

8

Alternative dates

The following may be celebrated on the alternative dates indicated:

Thomas the Apostle
– on 21 December 2019 instead of 3 July 2020

Matthias the Apostle
– on 24 February instead of 14 May

The Visit of the Blessed Virgin Mary to Elizabeth
– on 2 July instead of 1 June (transferred from 31 May)

Cuthbert
– on 4 September instead of 20 March

The Blessed Virgin Mary
– on 8 September instead of 15 August

Chad
– with Cedd on 26 October instead of 2 March

If any of the four festivals is celebrated on the alternative date these provisions should be used on the principal date:

Holy Communion	Morning Prayer	Evening Prayer
If Thomas the Apostle is celebrated on Saturday 21 December 2019 the following provision is used on Friday 3 July 2020:		
Amos 8.4–6, 9–12	Psalm 55	Psalm 69
Psalm 119.1–8	Judges 11.29–end	Job 31
Matthew 9.9–13	Luke 17.1–10	Romans 13.8–end
If Matthias the Apostle is celebrated on Monday 24 February the following provision is used on Thursday 14 May:		
Acts 15.7–21	Psalms 57, 148 or 78.1–39*	Psalm 104 or 78.40–end*
Psalm 96.1–3, 7–10	Numbers 13.1–3, 17–end	Deuteronomy 19
John 15.9–11	Luke 5.27–end	1 Peter 2.11–end
If The Visit of the Blessed Virgin Mary to Elizabeth is celebrated on Thursday 2 July following provision is used on Monday 1 June:		
2 Peter 1.2–7	Psalms 123, 124, 125, 126	Psalms 127, 128, 129
Psalm 91.1–2, 14–end	Joshua 1	Job 1
Mark 12.1–12	Luke 9.18–27	Romans 1.1–17
If The Blessed Virgin Mary is celebrated on Tuesday 8 September the following provision is used on Saturday 15 August:		
Ezekiel 18.1–11a, 13b, 30, 32	Psalm 68	Psalms 65, 66
Psalm 51.1–3, 15–17	1 Samuel 23	Ezekiel 47.1–12
Matthew 19.13–15	Acts 3.1–10	Mark 2.13–22

Key to the Tables

For guidance on how the options for saying the psalms are expressed typographically, see page 5.

Sundays (and Principal Feasts, other Principal Holy Days, and Festivals)

		Principal Service	3rd Service	2nd Service
Day	**Date** Sunday / Feast † / Festival ††	*Colour*	Main service of the day: Holy Communion, Morning Prayer, Evening Prayer, or a Service of the Word	Shorter Readings, an Office lectionary probably used at Morning Prayer where Holy Communion is the Principal Service	2nd main service, probably used at Evening Prayer; adaptable for Holy Communion

† Principal Feasts and other Principal Holy Days are printed in **bold**.
†† Festivals are printed in roman typeface.

Weekdays

		Holy Communion	Morning Prayer	Evening Prayer
Day	**Date**	*Colour*	Weekday readings	Psalms and readings for Morning Prayer	Psalms and readings for Evening Prayer

Lesser Festival ‡* [optional]
Commemoration ‡‡ [optional]

‡ Lesser Festivals are printed in roman typeface, in black.
‡‡ Commemorations are printed in *italics*.
* The ascriptions given to holy men and women in the Calendar (such as martyr, teacher of the faith, etc.) have often been abbreviated in this booklet for reasons of space. The particular ascription given is there to be helpful if needing to choose Collects and readings from Common of the Saints; where several ascriptions are used (e.g. bishop and martyr), traditionally the last ascription given is the most important and therefore the guiding one. The full ascriptions may be found in the Calendar, which is printed in *Common Worship: Times and Seasons* (pages 7–22), *Common Worship: Festivals* (pages 5–20) and *Common Worship: Daily Prayer* (pages 5–16). These incorporate minor corrections made since the publication of the Calendar in *Common Worship: Services and Prayers for the Church of England* (pages 5–16).

9

10

		Principal Service	3rd Service	2nd Service
Sunday	**1 December** *P* **1st Sunday of Advent**	Isaiah 2.1–5 Psalm 122 Romans 13.11–end Matthew 24.36–44	Psalm 44 Micah 4.1–7 1 Thessalonians 5.1–11	Psalm 9 [or 9.1–8] Isaiah 52.1–12 Matthew 24.15–28
		Holy Communion	Morning Prayer	Evening Prayer
Monday	**2 December** *P*	Isaiah 4.2–end Psalm 122 Matthew 8.5–11	Psalms **50**, 54 or 1, 2, 3 Isaiah 25.1–9 Matthew 12.1–21	Psalms 70, **71** or **4**, 7 Isaiah 42.18–end Revelation 19
Tuesday	**3 December** *P* *Francis Xavier, missionary, 1552*	Isaiah 11.1–10 Psalm 72.1–4, 18–19 Luke 10.21–24	Psalms **80**, 82 or **5**, 6 (8) Isaiah 26.1–13 Matthew 12.22–37	Psalms **74**, 75 or **9**, 10* Isaiah 43.1–13 Revelation 20
Wednesday	**4 December** *P* *John of Damascus, monk,* *teacher of the faith, c.749* *Nicholas Ferrar, deacon, founder of the* *Little Gidding Community, 1637*	Isaiah 25.6–10a Psalm 23 Matthew 15.29–37	Psalms 5, **7** or 119.**1**–**32** Isaiah 28.1–13 Matthew 12.38–end	Psalms 76, **77** or **11**, 12, 13 Isaiah 43.14–end Revelation 21.1–8
Thursday	**5 December** *P*	Isaiah 26.1–6 Psalm 118.18–27a Matthew 7.21, 24–27	Psalms **42**, 43 or 14, **15**, 16 Isaiah 28.14–end Matthew 13.1–23	Psalms **40**, 46 or **18*** Isaiah 44.1–8 Revelation 21.9–21
Friday	**6 December** *Pw* *Nicholas, bishop, c.326 (see p.81)*	Isaiah 29.17–end Psalm 27.1–4, 16–17 Matthew 9.27–31	Psalms **25**, 26 or 17, **19** Isaiah 29.1–14 Matthew 13.24–43	Psalms 16, **17** or **22** Isaiah 44.9–23 Revelation 21.22—22.5
Saturday	**7 December** *Pw* *Ambrose, bishop,* *teacher of the faith, 397 (see p.80)*	Isaiah 30.19–21, 23–26 Psalm 146.4–9 Matthew 9.35—10.1, 6–8	Psalms **9** (10) or 20, 21, **23** Isaiah 29.15–end Matthew 13.44–end	Psalms **27**, 28 or **24**, 25 Isaiah 44.24–45.13 Revelation 22.6–end

		Principal Service	3rd Service	2nd Service
Sunday	**8 December** *P* **2nd Sunday of Advent**	Isaiah 11.1–10 Psalm 72.1–7, 18–19 [or 72.1–7] Romans 15.4–13 Matthew 3.1–12	Psalm 80 Amos 7 Luke 1.5–20	Psalms 11 [28] 1 Kings 18.17–39 John 1.19–28
		Holy Communion	*Morning Prayer*	*Evening Prayer*
Monday	**9 December** *P*	Isaiah 35 Psalm 85.7–end Luke 5.17–26	Psalm 44 *or* 27, **30** Isaiah 30.1–18 Matthew 14.1–12	Psalms **144**, 146 *or* 26, **28**, 29 Isaiah 45.14–end 1 Thessalonians 1
Tuesday	**10 December** *P*	Isaiah 40.1–11 Psalm 96.1, 10–end Matthew 18.12–14	Psalms **56**, 57 *or* 32, **36** Isaiah 30.19–end Matthew 14.13–end	Psalms **11**, 12, 13 *or* **33** Isaiah 46 1 Thessalonians 2.1–12
Wednesday	**11 December** Ember Day	Isaiah 40.25–end Psalm 103.8–13 Matthew 11.28–end	Psalms **62**, 63 *or* **34** Isaiah 31 Matthew 15.1–20	Psalms **10**, 14 *or* 119.**33–56** Isaiah 47 1 Thessalonians 2.13–end
Thursday	**12 December** *P*	Isaiah 41.13–20 Psalm 145.1, 8–13 Matthew 11.11–15	Psalms 53, **54**, 60 *or* **37*** Isaiah 32 Matthew 15.21–28	Psalm **73** *or* 39, **40** Isaiah 48.1–11 1 Thessalonians 3
Friday	**13 December** *Pr* Lucy, martyr, 304 (see p.79) *Samuel Johnson, moralist, 1784* Ember Day	Isaiah 48.17–19 Psalm 1 Matthew 11.16–19	Psalms 85, **86** *or* **31** Isaiah 33.1–22 Matthew 15.29–end	Psalms 82, **90** *or* **35** Isaiah 48.12–end 1 Thessalonians 4.1–12
Saturday	**14 December** *Pw* John of the Cross, poet, teacher of the faith, 1591 (see p.80) Ember Day	Ecclesiasticus 48.1–4, 9–11 *or* 2 Kings 2.9–12 Psalm 80.1–4, 18–19 Matthew 17.10–13	Psalm **145** *or* 41, **42**, 43 Isaiah 35 Matthew 16.1–12	Psalms 93, **94** *or* 45, **46** Isaiah 49.1–13 1 Thessalonians 4.13–end

Advent 3

		Principal Service	3rd Service	2nd Service
Sunday	**15 December** P **3rd Sunday of Advent**	Isaiah 35.1–10 Psalm 146.4–10 or *Canticle:* Magnificat James 5.7–10 Matthew 11.2–11	Psalm 68.1–19 Zephaniah 3.14–20 Philippians 4.4–7	Psalm 12 [14] Isaiah 5.8–end Acts 13.13–41 HC John 5.31–40
		Holy Communion	**Morning Prayer**	**Evening Prayer**
Monday	**16 December** P	Numbers 24.2–7, 15–17 Psalm 25.3–8 Matthew 21.23–27	Psalm 40 or 44 Isaiah 38.1–8, 21–22 Matthew 16.13–end	Psalms 25, **26** or **47**, 49 Isaiah 49.14–25 1 Thessalonians 5.1–11
Tuesday	**17 December** P *O Sapientia* Eglantyne Jebb, social reformer, *founder of 'Save The Children', 1928*	Genesis 49.2, 8–10 Psalm 72.1–5, 18–19 Matthew 1.1–17	Psalm **70**, 74 or **48**, 52 Isaiah 38.9–20 Matthew 17.1–13	Psalms **50**, 54 or **50** Isaiah 50 1 Thessalonians 5.12–end
Wednesday	**18 December** P	Jeremiah 23.5–8 Psalm 72.1–2, 12–13, 18–end Matthew 1.18–24	Psalms **75**, 96 or 119.**57–80** Isaiah 39 Matthew 17.14–21	Psalms 25, **82** or **59**, 60 (67) Isaiah 51.1–8 2 Thessalonians 1
			From Thursday 19 December until the Epiphany the seasonal psalmody must be used at Morning and Evening Prayer	
Thursday	**19 December** P	Judges 13.2–7, 24–end Psalm 71.3–8 Luke 1.5–25	Psalms 144, **146** Zephaniah 1.1—2.3 Matthew 17.22–end	Psalms 10, **57** Isaiah 51.9–16 2 Thessalonians 2
Friday	**20 December** P	Isaiah 7.10–14 Psalm 24.1–6 Luke 1.26–38	Psalms 46, 95 Zephaniah 3.1–13 Matthew 18.1–20	Psalms 4, 9 Isaiah 51.17–end 2 Thessalonians 3
Saturday	**21 December** P	Zephaniah 3.14–18 Psalm 33.1–4, 11–12, 20–end Luke 1.39–45	Psalms 121, 122, 123 Zephaniah 3.14–end Matthew 18.21–end	Psalms 80, **84** Isaiah 52.1–12 Jude

		Principal Service	3rd Service	2nd Service
Sunday	**22 December** *P* **4th Sunday of Advent**	Isaiah 7.10–16 / Psalm 80.1–8, 18–20 [or 80.1–8] / Romans 1.1–7 / Matthew 1.18–end	Psalm 144 / Micah 5.2–5a / Luke 1.26–38	Psalms 113 [126] / 1 Samuel 1.1–20 / Revelation 22.6–end / HC Luke 1.39–45
		Holy Communion	**Morning Prayer**	**Evening Prayer**
Monday	**23 December** *P*	Malachi 3.1–4, 4.5–end / Psalm 25.3–9 / Luke 1.57–66	Psalms 128, 129, **130**, 131 / Malachi 1.1, 6–end / Matthew 19.1–12	Psalm **89**.1–37 / Isaiah 52.13—end of 53 / 2 Peter 1.1–15
Tuesday	**24 December** *P* **Christmas Eve**	2 Samuel 7.1–5, 8–11, 16 / Psalm 89.2, 19–27 / Acts 13.16–26 / Luke 1.67–79	Psalms **45**, 113 / Malachi 2.1–16 / Matthew 19.13–15	Psalm **85** / Zechariah 2 / Revelation 1.1–8
		Principal Service	**3rd Service**	**2nd Service**
Wednesday	**25 December** *Gold or W* **Christmas Day**	*Any of the following three sets of Principal Service readings may be used on the evening of Christmas Eve and on Christmas Day. Set III should be used at some service during the celebration.* **Set I** Isaiah 9.2–7 / Psalm 96 / Titus 2.11–14 / Luke 2.1–14 [15–20] **Set II** Isaiah 62.6–end / Psalm 97 / Titus 3.4–7 / Luke 2.[1–7] 8–20 **Set III** Isaiah 52.7–10 / Psalm 98 / Hebrews 1.1–4 [5–12] / John 1.1–14	MP Psalms **110**, 117 / Isaiah 62.1–5 / Matthew 1.18–end	EP Psalm 8 / Isaiah 65.17–25 / Philippians 2.5–11 *or Luke 2.1–20 if it has not been used at the principal service of the day*
Thursday	**26 December** *R* Stephen, deacon, first martyr	2 Chronicles 24.20–22 *or* Acts 7.51–end / Psalm 119.161–168 / Acts 7.51–end *or* Galatians 2.16b–20 / Matthew 10.17–22	MP Psalms **13**, 31.1–8, 150 / Jeremiah 26.12–15 / Acts 6	EP Psalms 57, **86** / Genesis 4.1–10 / Matthew 23.34–end
Friday	**27 December** *W* John, Apostle and Evangelist	Exodus 33.7–11a / Psalm 117 / 1 John 1 / John 21.19b–end	MP Psalms **21**, 147.13–end / Exodus 33.12–end / 1 John 2.1–11	EP Psalm **97** / Isaiah 6.1–8 / 1 John 5.1–12
Saturday	**28 December** *R* The Holy Innocents	Jeremiah 31.15–17 / Psalm 124 / 1 Corinthians 1.26–29 / Matthew 2.13–18	MP Psalms **36**, 146 / Baruch 4.21–27 *or* Genesis 37.13–20 / Matthew 18.1–10	EP Psalms 123, **128** / Isaiah 49.14–25 / Mark 10.13–16

Christmas 1

		Principal Service	3rd Service	2nd Service
Sunday **29 December** 1st Sunday of Christmas	W	Isaiah 63.7–9 Psalm 148 [or 148.7–end] Hebrews 2.10–end Matthew 2.13–end	Psalm 105.1–11 Isaiah 35.1–6 Galatians 3.23–end	Psalm 132 Isaiah 49.7–13 Philippians 2.1–11 HC Luke 2.41–52
		Holy Communion	**Morning Prayer**	**Evening Prayer**
Monday **30 December**	W	1 John 2.12–17 Psalm 96.7–10 Luke 2.36–40	Psalms 111, 112, **113** Jonah 2 Colossians 1.15–23	Psalms **65**, 84 Isaiah 59.1–15a John 1.19–28
Tuesday **31 December** John Wyclif, reformer, 1384	W	1 John 2.18–21 Psalm 96.1, 11–end John 1.1–18	Psalm **102** Jonah 3–4 Colossians 1.24—2.7	Psalms **90**, 148 Isaiah 59.15b–end John 1.29–34 *or:* 1st EP of the Naming and Circumcision of Jesus: Psalm 148; Jeremiah 23.1–6; Colossians 2.8–15
		Principal Service	**3rd Service**	**2nd Service**
Wednesday **1 January** Naming and Circumcision of Jesus	W	Numbers 6.22–end Psalm 8 Galatians 4.4–7 Luke 2.15–21	MP Psalms **103**, 150 Genesis 17.1–13 Romans 2.17–end	EP Psalm 115 Deuteronomy 30. [1–10] 11–end Acts 3.1–16
		Holy Communion	**Morning Prayer**	**Evening Prayer**
Thursday **2 January** Basil the Great and Gregory of Nazianzus, bishops, teachers of the faith, 379 and 389 (see p.80); *Seraphim, monk, spiritual guide, 1833* Vedanayagam Samuel Azariah, bishop, evangelist, 1945	W	1 John 2.22–28 Psalm **98**.1–4 John 1.19–28	Psalm **18**.1–30 Ruth 1 Colossians 2.8–end	Psalms 45, **46** Isaiah 60.1–12 John 1.35–42
Friday **3 January**	W	1 John 2.29—3.6 Psalm 98.2–7 John 1.29–34	Psalms **127**, 128, 131 Ruth 2 Colossians 3.1–11	Psalms **2**, 110 Isaiah 60.13–end John 1.43–end
Saturday **4 January**	W	1 John 3.7–10 Psalm 98.1, 8–end John 1.35–42	Psalm **89**.1–37 Ruth 3 Colossians 3.12—4.1	Psalms 85, **87** Isaiah 61 John 2.1–12 *or, if the Epiphany is celebrated on Sunday 5 January:* **1st EP of the Epiphany:** Psalms 96, **97**; Isaiah 49.1–13; John 4.7–26

Christmas 2 / Epiphany

If the Epiphany is celebrated on Monday 6 January:

			Principal Service	3rd Service	2nd Service
Sunday	**5 January** 2nd Sunday of Christmas	W	Jeremiah 31.7–14 or Ecclesiasticus 24.1–12 Psalm 147.13–end or *Canticle*: Wisdom of Solomon 10.15–end Ephesians 1.3–14 John 1.[1–9]10–18	Psalm 87 Jeremiah 31.15–17 2 Corinthians 1.3–12	1st EP of the Epiphany Psalms 96, **97** Isaiah 49.1–13 John 4.7–26
Monday	**6 January** Epiphany	Gold or W	Isaiah 60.1–6 Psalm 72.[1–9]10–15 Ephesians 3.1–12 Matthew 2.1–12	MP Psalms **132**, 113 Jeremiah 31.7–14 John 1.29–34	EP Psalms **98**, 100 Baruch 4.36—end of 5 or Isaiah 60.1–9 John 2.1–11

			Holy Communion	Morning Prayer	Evening Prayer
Tuesday	**7 January**	W	1 John 3.22—4.6 Psalm 2.7–end Matthew 4.12–17, 23–end	Psalms 99, 147.1–12 or **73** Baruch 1.15—2.10 or Jeremiah 23.1–8 Matthew 20.1–16	Psalm 118 or **74** Isaiah 63.7–end 1 John 3
Wednesday	**8 January**	W	1 John 4.7–10 Psalm 72.1–8 Mark 6.34–44	Psalms **46**, 147.13–end or **77** Baruch 2.11–end or Jeremiah 30.1–17 Matthew 20.17–28	Psalms **145** or 119.81–104 Isaiah 64 1 John 4.7–end
Thursday	**9 January**	W	1 John 4.11–18 Psalm 72.1, 10–13 Mark 6.45–52	Psalms 2, **148** or **78**.1–39* Baruch 3.1–8 or Jeremiah 30.18—31.9 Matthew 20.29–end	Psalms **67**, 72 or **78**.40–end* Isaiah 65.1–16 1 John 5.1–12
Friday	**10 January** *William Laud, archbishop, 1645*	W	1 John 4.19—5.4 Psalm 72.1, 17–end Luke 4.14–22	Psalms 97, **149** or 55 Baruch 3.9—4.4 or Jeremiah 31.10–17 Matthew 23.1–12	Psalms 27, **29** or 69 Isaiah 65.17–end 1 John 5.13–end
Saturday	**11 January** *Mary Slessor, missionary, 1915*	W	1 John 5.5–13 Psalm 147.13–end Luke 5.12–16	Psalms 98, **150** or 76, **79** Baruch 4.21–30 or Jeremiah 33.14–end Matthew 23.13–28	1st EP of the Baptism of Christ Psalm 36 Isaiah 61 Titus 2.11–14; 3.4–7

15

Epiphany

If the Epiphany is celebrated on Sunday 5 January:

		Principal Service	3rd Service	2nd Service
Sunday 5 January Epiphany	Gold or W	Isaiah 60.1–6 Psalm 72. [1–9] 10–15 Ephesians 3.1–12 Matthew 2.1–12	MP Psalms **132**, 113 Jeremiah 31.7–14 John 1.29–34	EP Psalms **98**, 100 Baruch 4.36—end of 5 or Isaiah 60.1–9 John 2.1–11
		Holy Communion	Morning Prayer	Evening Prayer
Monday 6 January	W	1 John 3.22—4.6 Psalm 2.7—end Matthew 4.12–17, 23—end	Psalms 8, **48** or **71** Ruth 4.1–17 Colossians 4.2—end	Psalms 96, **97** or **72**, 75 Isaiah 62 John 2.13—end
Tuesday 7 January	W	1 John 4.7–10 Psalm 72.1–8 Mark 6.34–44	Psalms **99**, 147.1–12 or **73** Baruch 1.15—2.10 or Jeremiah 23.1–8 Matthew 20.1–16	Psalm **118** or **74** Isaiah 63.7—end 1 John 3
Wednesday 8 January	W	1 John 4.11–18 Psalm 72.1, 10–13 Mark 6.45–52	Psalms **46**, 147.13—end or **77** Baruch 2.11—end or Jeremiah 30.1–11 Matthew 20.17–28	Psalm **145** 72 or **119.81–104** Isaiah 64 1 John 4.7—end
Thursday 9 January	W	1 John 4.19—5.4 Psalm 72.1, 17—end Luke 4.14–22	Psalms 2, **148** or **78.1–39*** Baruch 3.1–8 or Jeremiah 30.18—31.9 Matthew 20.29—end	Psalms **67**, 72 or **78.40—end*** Isaiah 65.1–16 1 John 5.1–12
Friday 10 January *William Laud, archbishop, 1645*	W	1 John 5.5–13 Psalm 147.13—end Luke 5.12–16	Psalms 97, **149** or **55** Baruch 3.9—4.4 or Jeremiah 31.10–17 Matthew 23.1–12	Psalms 27, **29** or **69** Isaiah 65.17—end 1 John 5.13—end
Saturday 11 January *Mary Slessor, missionary, 1915*	W	1 John 5.14—end Psalm 149.1–5 John 3.22–30	Psalms 98, **150** or **76**, 79 Baruch 4.21–30 or Jeremiah 33.14—end Matthew 23.13–28	**1st EP of the Baptism of Christ** Psalm 36 Isaiah 61 Titus 2.11—14; 3.4–7

Baptism of Christ (Epiphany 1)

			Principal Service	3rd Service	2nd Service
Sunday	**12 January** **Baptism of Christ** 1st Sunday of Epiphany	Gold or W	Isaiah 42.1–9 Psalm 29 Acts 10.34–43 Matthew 3.13–end	Psalm 89.19–29 Exodus 14.15–22 1 John 5.6–9	Psalms 46, 47 Joshua 3.1–8,14–end Hebrews 1.1–12 HC Luke 3.15–22
			Holy Communion	*Morning Prayer*	*Evening Prayer*
Monday	**13 January** Hilary, bishop, teacher of the faith, 367 (see p.80) Kentigern (Mungo), missionary bishop, 603 George Fox, founder of the Society of Friends (Quakers), 1691 DEL week 1	W	1 Samuel 1.1–8 Psalm 116. 10–15 Mark 1.14–20	Psalms **2**, 110 or **80**, 82 Genesis 1.1–19 Matthew 21.1–17	Psalms **34**, 36 or **85**, 86 Amos 1 1 Corinthians 1.1–17
Tuesday	**14 January**	W	1 Samuel 1.9–20 *Canticle:* 1 Samuel 2.1, 4–8 or Magnificat Mark 1.21–28	Psalms **8**, 9 or 87, **89.1–18** Genesis 1.20—2.3 Matthew 21.18–32	Psalms **45**, 46 or **89.19–end** Amos 2 1 Corinthians 1.18–end
Wednesday	**15 January**	W	1 Samuel 3.1–10, 19–20 Psalm 40.1–4, 7–10 Mark 1.29–39	Psalms 19, **20** or 119.**105–128** Genesis 2.4–end Matthew 21.33–end	Psalms **47**, 48 or **91**, 93 Amos 3 1 Corinthians 2
Thursday	**16 January**	W	1 Samuel 4.1–11 Psalm 44.10–15, 24–25 Mark 1.40–end	Psalms **21**, 24 or 90, **92** Genesis 3 Matthew 22.1–14	Psalms **61**, 65 or **94** Amos 4 1 Corinthians 3
Friday	**17 January** Antony of Egypt, hermit, abbot, 356 (see p.82) Charles Gore, bishop, founder of the Community of the Resurrection, 1932	W	1 Samuel 8.4–7, 10–end Psalm 89.15–18 Mark 2.1–12	Psalms **67**, 72 or **88** (95) Genesis 4.1–16, 25–26 Matthew 22.15–33	Psalm **68** or **102** Amos 5.1–17 1 Corinthians 4
Saturday	**18 January** **Week of Prayer for Christian Unity:** **18–25 January** Amy Carmichael, founder of the Dohnavur Fellowship, spiritual writer, 1951	W	1 Samuel 9.1–4, 17–19, 10.1*a* Psalm 21.1–6 Mark 2.13–17	Psalms 29, **33** or 96, **97**, 100 Genesis 6.1–10 Matthew 22.34–end	Psalms 84, **85** or **104** Amos 5.18–end 1 Corinthians 5

Epiphany 2

		Principal Service	3rd Service	2nd Service
Sunday	19 January W **2nd Sunday of Epiphany**	Isaiah 49.1–7 Psalm 40.1–12 1 Corinthians 1.1–9 John 1.29–42	Psalm 145.1–12 Jeremiah 1.4–10 Mark 1.14–20	Psalm 96 Ezekiel 2.1—3.4 Galatians 1.11–end HC John 1.43–end
		Holy Communion	**Morning Prayer**	**Evening Prayer**
Monday	20 January W *Richard Rolle, spiritual writer, 1349* DEL week 2	1 Samuel 15.16–23 Psalm 50.8–10, 16–17, 24 Mark 2.18–22	Psalms 145, **146** or **98**, 99, 101 Genesis 6.11—7.10 Matthew 24.1–14	Psalm 71 or 105* (or 103) Amos 6 1 Corinthians 6.1–11
Tuesday	21 January Wr *Agnes, child martyr, 304* (see p.79)	1 Samuel 16.1–13 Psalm 89.19–27 Mark 2.23–end	Psalms **132**, 147.1–12 or **106*** (or 103) Genesis 7.11–end Matthew 24.15–28	Psalm **89.1–37** or **107*** Amos 7 1 Corinthians 6.12–end
Wednesday	22 January W *Vincent of Saragossa, deacon, martyr, 304*	1 Samuel 17.32–33, 37, 40–51 Psalm 144.1–2, 9–10 Mark 3.1–6	Psalms **81**, 147.13–end or 110, **111**, 112 Genesis 8.1–14 Matthew 24.29–end	Psalms **97**, 98 or **119.129–152** Amos 8 1 Corinthians 7.1–24
Thursday	23 January W	1 Samuel 18.6–9; 19.1–7 Psalm 56.1–2, 8–end Mark 3.7–12	Psalms **76**, 148 or 113, **115** Genesis 8.15—9.7 Matthew 25.1–13	Psalms 99, 100, **111** or 114, **116**, 117 Amos 9 1 Corinthians 7.25–end
Friday	24 January W *Francis de Sales, bishop,* *teacher of the faith, 1622* (see p.80)	1 Samuel 24.3–22*a* Psalm 57.1–2, 8–end Mark 3.13–19	Psalms **27**, 149 or **139** Genesis 9.8–19 Matthew 25.14–30	Psalm **73** or **130**, 131, 137 Hosea 1.1—2.1 1 Corinthians 8 *or:* 1st EP of the Conversion of Paul: Psalm 149; Isaiah 49.1–13; Acts 22.3–16
		Principal Service	**3rd Service**	**2nd Service**
Saturday	25 January W Conversion of Paul	Jeremiah 1.4–10 or Acts 9.1–22 Psalm 67 Acts 9.1–22 or Galatians 1.11–16*a* Matthew 19.27–end	MP Psalms 66, 147.13–end Ezekiel 3.22–end Philippians 3.1–14	EP Psalm 119.41–56 Ecclesiasticus 39.1–10 or Isaiah 56.1–8 Colossians 1.24—2.7

Epiphany 3

		Principal Service	3rd Service	2nd Service
Sunday	26 January W **3rd Sunday of Epiphany**	Isaiah 9.1–4 Psalm 27.1, 4–12 [or 27.1–11] 1 Corinthians 1.10–18 Matthew 4.12–23	Psalm 113 Amos 3.1–8 1 John 1.1–4	Psalm 33 [or 33.1–12] Ecclesiastes 3.1–11 1 Peter 1.3–12 HC Luke 4.14–21
		Holy Communion	**Morning Prayer**	**Evening Prayer**
Monday	27 January W DEL week 3	2 Samuel 5.1–7, 10 Psalm 89.19–27 Mark 3. 22–30	Psalms 40, **108** or 123, 124, 125, **126** Genesis 11.27—12.9 Matthew 26.1–16	Psalms **138**, 144 or **127**, 128, 129 Hosea 2.18—end of 3 1 Corinthians 9.15–end
Tuesday	28 January W Thomas Aquinas, priest, philosopher, teacher of the faith, 1274 (see p.80)	2 Samuel 6.12–15, 17–19 Psalm 24.7–end Mark 3.31–end	Psalms 34.**36** or **132**, 133 Genesis 13.2–end Matthew 26.17–35	Psalm **145** or (134,) **135** Hosea 4.1–16 1 Corinthians 10.1–13
Wednesday	29 January W	2 Samuel 7.4–17 Psalm 89.19–27 Mark 4.1–20	Psalms 45, **46** or **119.153–end** Genesis 14 Matthew 26.36–46	Psalms 21, **29** or **136** Hosea 5.1–7 1 Corinthians 10.14—11.1
Thursday	30 January Wr Charles, king and martyr, 1649 (see p.79)	2 Samuel 7.18–19, 24–end Psalm 132.1–5, 11–15 Mark 4.21–25	Psalms **47**, 48 or **143**, 146 Genesis 15 Matthew 26.47–56	Psalms **24**, 33 or **138**, 140, 141 Hosea 5.8—6.6 1 Corinthians 11.2–16
Friday	31 January W John Bosco, priest, founder of the Salesian Teaching Order, 1888	2 Samuel 11.1–10, 13–17 Psalm 51.1–6, 9 Mark 4.26–34	Psalms 61, **65** or 142, **144** Genesis 16 Matthew 26.57–end	Psalms **67**, 77 or **145** Hosea 6.7—7.2 1 Corinthians 11.17–end
Saturday	1 February W Brigid, abbess, c.525	2 Samuel 12.1–7, 10–17 Psalm 51.11–16 Mark 4.35–end	Psalm **68** or **147** Genesis 17.1–22 Matthew 27.1–10	**1st EP of the Presentation** Psalm 118 1 Samuel 1.19b–end Hebrews 4.11–end

Presentation

			Principal Service	3rd Service	2nd Service
Sunday	**2 February** Presentation of Christ in the Temple (Candlemas)	*Gold or W*	Malachi 3.1–5 Psalm 24.[1–6]7–end Hebrews 2.14–end Luke 2.22–40	MP Psalms **48**, 146 Exodus 13.1–16 Romans 12.1–5	EP Psalms 122, **132** Haggai 2.1–9 John 2.18–22
			Holy Communion	Morning Prayer	Evening Prayer
Monday	**3 February** Anskar, archbishop, missionary, 865 (see p.82) Ordinary Time starts today The Collect of 5 before Lent is used DEL week 4	*Gw*	2 Samuel 15.13–14, 30, 16.5–13 Psalm 3 Mark 5.1–20	Psalms **1**, 2, 3 Leviticus 19.1–18, 30–end 1 Timothy 1.1–17	Psalms **4**, 7 Joel 1.1–14 John 15.1–11
Tuesday	**4 February** *Gilbert, founder of the Gilbertine Order, 1189*	*G*	2 Samuel 18.9–10, 14, 24–25, 30—19.3 Psalm 86.1–6 Mark 5.21–end	Psalms **5**, 6 (8) Leviticus 23.1–22 1 Timothy 1.18—end of 2	Psalms **9**, 10* Joel 1.15–end John 15.12–17
Wednesday	**5 February**	*G*	2 Samuel 24.2, 9–17 Psalm 32.1–8 Mark 6.1–6a	Psalm 119.**1**–32 Leviticus 23.23–end 1 Timothy 3	Psalms **11**, 12, 13 Joel 2.1–11 John 15.18–end
Thursday	**6 February** *Martyrs of Japan, 1597* *Accession of Queen Elizabeth II, 1952* (see p.85)	*G*	1 Kings 2.1–4, 10–12 *Canticle:* 1 Chronicles 29.10–12 or Psalm 145.1–5 Mark 6.7–13	Psalms 14, **15**, 16 Leviticus 24.1–9 1 Timothy 4	Psalm **18*** Joel 2.18–27 John 16.1–15
Friday	**7 February**	*G*	Ecclesiasticus 47.2–11 Psalm 18.31–36, 50–end Mark 6.14–29	Psalms 17, **19** Leviticus 25.1–24 1 Timothy 5.1–16	Psalm **22** Joel 2.28–end John 16.16–22
Saturday	**8 February**	*G*	1 Kings 3.4–13 Psalm 119.9–16 Mark 6.30–34	Psalms 20, 21, **23** Numbers 6.1–5, 21–end 1 Timothy 5.17–end	Psalms **24**, 25 Joel 3.1–3, 9–end John 16.23–end

		Principal Service	3rd Service	2nd Service
Sunday	9 February 3rd Sunday before Lent Proper 1 G	Isaiah 58.1–9a [9b–12] Psalm 112 [or 112.1–9] 1 Corinthians 2.1–12 [13–end] Matthew 5.13–20	Psalms 5, 6 Jeremiah 26.1–16 Acts 3.1–10	Psalms [1, 3] 4 Amos 2.4–end Ephesians 4.17–end HC Mark 1.29–39
		Holy Communion	Morning Prayer	Evening Prayer
Monday	10 February G *Scholastica, abbess, c.543* DEL week 5	1 Kings 8.1–7, 9–13 Psalm 132.1–9 Mark 6.53–end	Psalms 27, **30** Genesis 24.1–28 1 Timothy 6.1–10	Psalms 26, **28**, 29 Ecclesiastes 1 John 17.1–5
Tuesday	11 February G	1 Kings 8.22–23, 27–30 Psalm 84.1–10 Mark 7.1–13	Psalms 32, **36** Genesis 24.29–end 1 Timothy 6.11–end	Psalm 33 Ecclesiastes 2 John 17.6–19
Wednesday	12 February G	1 Kings 10.1–10 Psalm 37.3–6, 30–32 Mark 7.14–23	Psalm 34 Genesis 25.7–11, 19–end 2 Timothy 1.1–14	Psalm **119.33–56** Ecclesiastes 3.1–15 John 17.20–end
Thursday	13 February G	1 Kings 11.4–13 Psalm 106.3, 35–41 Mark 7.24–30	Psalm 37* Genesis 26.34—27.40 2 Timothy 1.15—2.13	Psalms 39, 40 Ecclesiastes 3.16—end of 4 John 18.1–11
Friday	14 February Gw Cyril and Methodius, missionaries, 869 and 885 (see p.82) *Valentine, martyr at Rome, c.269*	1 Kings 11.29–32; 12.19 Psalm 81.8–14 Mark 7.31–end	Psalm 31 Genesis 27.41—end of 28 2 Timothy 2.14–end	Psalm 35 Ecclesiastes 5 John 18.12–27
Saturday	15 February G *Sigfrid, bishop, 1045* *Thomas Bray, priest,* *founder of SPCK and SPG, 1730*	1 Kings 12.26–32; 13.33–end Psalm 106.6–7, 20–23 Mark 8.1–10	Psalms 41, **42**, 43 Genesis 29.1–30 2 Timothy 3	Psalms **45**, 46 Ecclesiastes 6 John 18.28–end

			Principal Service	3rd Service	2nd Service
Sunday	16 February 2nd Sunday before Lent	G	Genesis 1.1—2.3 Psalm 136 [Psalm 136.1—9, 23—end] Romans 8.18—25 Matthew 6.25—end	Psalms 100, 150 Job 38.1—21 Colossians 1.15—20	Psalm 148 Proverbs 8.1, 22—31 Revelation 4 HC Luke 12.16—31

			Holy Communion	Morning Prayer	Evening Prayer
Monday	17 February Janani Luwum, archbishop, martyr, 1977 (see p.79) DEL week 6	Gr	James 1.1—11 Psalm 119.65—72 Mark 8.11—13	Psalm **44** Genesis 29.31—30.24 2 Timothy 4.1—8	Psalms **47**, 49 Ecclesiastes 7.1—14 John 19.1—16
Tuesday	18 February	G	James 1.12—18 Psalm 94.12—18 Mark 8.14—21	Psalms **48**, 52 Genesis 31.1—24 2 Timothy 4.9—end	Psalm **50** Ecclesiastes 7.15—end John 19.17—30
Wednesday	19 February	G	James 1.19—end Psalm 15 Mark 8.22—26	Psalm 1**19.57—80** Genesis 31.25—32.2 Titus 1	Psalm **59**, 60 (67) Ecclesiastes 8 John 19.31—end
Thursday	20 February	G	James 2.1—9 Psalm 34.1—7 Mark 8.27—33	Psalms 56, **57** (63*) Genesis 32.3—30 Titus 2	Psalms 61, **62**, 64 Ecclesiastes 9 John 20.1—10
Friday	21 February	G	James 2.14—24, 26 Psalm 112 Mark 8.34—9.1	Psalms **51**, 54 Genesis 33.1—17 Titus 3	Psalm **38** Ecclesiastes 11.1—8 John 20.11—18
Saturday	22 February	G	James 3.1—10 Psalm 12.1—7 Mark 9.2—13	Psalm **68** Genesis 35 Philemon	Psalms 65, **66** Ecclesiastes 11.9—end of 12 John 20.19—end

Sunday next before Lent

		Principal Service	3rd Service	2nd Service
Sunday	**23 February** **Sunday next before Lent** G	Exodus 24.12–end Psalm 2 [or Psalm 99] 2 Peter 1.16–end Matthew 17.1–9	Psalm 72 Exodus 34.29–end 2 Corinthians 4.3–6	Psalm 84 Ecclesiasticus 48.1–10 or 2 Kings 2.1–12 Matthew 17.9–23 (or 17.1–23)
		Holy Communion	Morning Prayer	Evening Prayer
Monday	**24 February** DEL week 7 G	James 3.13–end Psalm 19.7–end Mark 9.14–29	Psalm 71 Genesis 37.1–11 Galatians 1	Psalms 72, 75 Jeremiah 1 John 3.1–21
Tuesday	**25 February** G	James 4.1–10 Psalm 55.7–9, 24 Mark 9.30–37	Psalm 73 Genesis 37.12–end Galatians 2.1–10	Psalm 74 Jeremiah 2.1–13 John 3.22–end
		Principal Service	3rd Service	2nd Service
Wednesday	**26 February** **Ash Wednesday** P(La)	Joel 2.1–2, 12–17 or Isaiah 58.1–12 Psalm 51.1–18 2 Corinthians 5.20b—6.10 Matthew 6.1–6, 16–21 or John 8.1–11	MP Psalm 38 Daniel 9.3–6, 17–19 1 Timothy 6.6–19	EP Psalm 51 or 102 [or 102.1–18] Isaiah 1.10–18 Luke 15.11–end
		Holy Communion	Morning Prayer	Evening Prayer
Thursday	**27 February** George Herbert, priest, poet, 1633 (see p.81) P(La)w	Deuteronomy 30.15–end Psalm 1 Luke 9.22–25	Psalm 77 or 78.1–39* Genesis 39 Galatians 2.11–end	Psalm 74 or **78.40–end*** Jeremiah 2.14–32 John 4.1–26
Friday	**28 February** P(La)	Isaiah 58.1–9a Psalm 51.1–5, 17–18 Matthew 9.14–15	Psalms 3, 7 or 55 Genesis 40 Galatians 3.1–14	Psalm 31 or 69 Jeremiah 3.6–22 John 4.27–42
Saturday	**29 February** P(La)	Isaiah 58.9b–end Psalm 86.1–7 Luke 5.27–32	Psalm 71 or 76, 79 Genesis 41.1–24 Galatians 3.15–22	Psalm 73 or 81, 84 Jeremiah 4.1–18 John 4.43–end

Lent 1

			Principal Service	3rd Service	2nd Service
			Holy Communion	**Morning Prayer**	**Evening Prayer**
Sunday	**1 March** **1st Sunday of Lent**	*P(La)*	Genesis 2.15–17; 3.1–7 Psalm 32 Romans 5.12–19 Matthew 4.1–11	Psalm 119.1–16 Jeremiah 18.1–11 Luke 18.9–14	Psalm 50.1–15 Deuteronomy 6.4–9, 16–end Luke 15.1–10
Monday	**2 March** Chad, bishop, missionary, 672 (see p.82)	*P(La)w*	Leviticus 19.1–2, 11–18 Psalm 19.7–end Matthew 25.31–end	Psalms 10, 11 or **80**, 82 Genesis 41.25–45 Galatians 3.23—4.7	Psalms 12, **13**, 14 or **85**, 86 Jeremiah 4.19–end John 5.1–18
Tuesday	**3 March**	*P(La)*	Isaiah 55.10–11 Psalm 34.4–6, 21–22 Matthew 6.7–15	Psalm **44** or 87, **89.1–18** Genesis 41.46—42.5 Galatians 4.8–20	Psalms 46, **49** or **89.19–end** Jeremiah 5.1–19 John 5.19–29
Wednesday	**4 March** Ember Day	*P(La)*	Jonah 3 Psalm 51.1–5, 17–18 Luke 11.29–32	Psalms **6**, 17 or 119.**105–128** Genesis 42.6–17 Galatians 4.21—5.1	Psalms 9, **28** or **91**, 93 Jeremiah 5.20–end John 5.30–end
Thursday	**5 March**	*P(La)*	Esther 14.1–5, 12–14 or Isaiah 55.6–9 Psalm 138 Matthew 7.7–12	Psalms **42**, 43 or 90, **92** Genesis 42.18–28 Galatians 5.2–15	Psalms 137, 138, **142** or **94** Jeremiah 6.9–21 John 6.1–15
Friday	**6 March** Ember Day	*P(La)*	Ezekiel 18.21–28 Psalm 130 Matthew 5.20–26	Psalm **22** or **88** (95) Genesis 42.29–end Galatians 5.16–end	Psalms 54, **55** or 102 Jeremiah 6.22–end John 6.16–27
Saturday	**7 March** Perpetua, Felicity and companions, martyrs, 203 (see p.79) Ember Day	*P(La)r*	Deuteronomy 26.16–end Psalm 119.1–8 Matthew 5.43–end	Psalms 59, **63** or 96, **97**, 100 Genesis 43.1–15 Galatians 6	Psalms **4**, 16 or **104** Jeremiah 7.1–20 John 6.27–40

Lent 2

		Principal Service	3rd Service	2nd Service
Sunday	8 March P(La) 2nd Sunday of Lent	Genesis 12.1–4a Psalm 121 Romans 4.1–5, 13–17 John 3.1–17	Psalm 74 Jeremiah 22.1–9 Matthew 8.1–13	Psalm 135 [or 135.1–14] Numbers 21.4–9 Luke 14.27–33
		Holy Communion	**Morning Prayer**	**Evening Prayer**
Monday	9 March P(La)	Daniel 9.4–10 Psalm 79.8–9, 12, 14 Luke 6.36–38	Psalms 26, **32** or **98**, 99, 101 Genesis 43.16–end Hebrews 1	Psalms 70, **74** or **105*** (or 103) Jeremiah 7.21–end John 6.41–51
Tuesday	10 March P(La)	Isaiah 1.10, 16–20 Psalm 50.8, 16–end Matthew 23.1–12	Psalm **50** or **106*** (or 103) Genesis 44.1–17 Hebrews 2.1–9	Psalms **52**, 53, 54 or **107*** Jeremiah 8.1–15 John 6.52–59
Wednesday	11 March P(La)	Jeremiah 18.18–20 Psalm 31.4–5, 14–18 Matthew 20.17–28	Psalm **35** or 110, **111**, 112 Genesis 44.18–end Hebrews 2.10–end	Psalms 3, 51 or 119.**129–152** Jeremiah 8.18–9.11 John 6.60–end
Thursday	12 March P(La)	Jeremiah 17.5–10 Psalm 1 Luke 16.19–end	Psalm **34** or 113, **115** Genesis 45.1–15 Hebrews 3.1–6	Psalm **71** or 114, **116**, 117 Jeremiah 9.12–24 John 7.1–13
Friday	13 March P(La)	Genesis 37.3–4, 12–13, 17–28 Psalm 105.16–22 Matthew 21.33–43, 45–46	Psalms 40, **41** or **139** Genesis 45.16–end Hebrews 3.7–end	Psalms 6, 38 or **130**, 131, 137 Jeremiah 10.1–16 John 7.14–24
Saturday	14 March P(La)	Micah 7.14–15, 18–20 Psalm 103.1–4, 9–12 Luke 15.1–3, 11–end	Psalms 3, **25** or 120, **121**, 122 Genesis 46.1–7, 28–end Hebrews 4.1–13	Psalms **23**, 27 or **118** Jeremiah 10.17–24 John 7.25–36

Lent 3

			Principal Service	3rd Service	2nd Service
Sunday	**15 March** **3rd Sunday of Lent**	P(La)	Exodus 17.1–7 Psalm 95 Romans 5.1–11 John 4.5–42	Psalm 46 Amos 7.10–end 2 Corinthians 1.1–11	Psalm 40 Joshua 1.1–9 Ephesians 6.10–20 HC John 2.13–22
			Holy Communion	**Morning Prayer**	**Evening Prayer**

The following readings may replace those provided for Holy Communion on any day (except Joseph of Nazareth) during the Third Week of Lent: Exodus 17.1–7; Psalm 95.1–7; Psalm 95.1–2, 6–end; John 4.5–42

			Holy Communion	Morning Prayer	Evening Prayer
Monday	**16 March**	P(La)	2 Kings 5.1–15 Psalms 42.1–2; 43.1–4 Luke 4.24–30	Psalms 5, 7 or 123, 124, 125, **126** Genesis 47.1–27 Hebrews 4.14—5.10	Psalms 11, 17 or **127**, 128, 129 Jeremiah 11.1–17 John 7.37–52
Tuesday	**17 March** Patrick, bishop, missionary, patron of Ireland, c.460 (see p.82)	P(La)w	Song of the Three 2, 11–20 or Daniel 2.20–23 Psalm 25.3–10 Matthew 18.21–end	Psalms 6, **9** or **132**, 133 Genesis 47.28—end of 48 Hebrews 5.11—6.12	Psalms 61, 62, **64** or (134,) **135** Jeremiah 11.18—12.6 John 7.53—8.11
Wednesday	**18 March** *Cyril, bishop, teacher of the faith, 386*	P(La)	Deuteronomy 4.1, 5–9 Psalm 147.13–end Matthew 5.17–19	Psalm **38** or **119.153–end** Genesis 49.1–32 Hebrews 6.13–end	Psalms 36, **39** or **136** Jeremiah 13.1–11 John 8.12–30 or: 1st EP of Joseph of Nazareth: Psalm 132; Hosea 11.1–9; Luke 2.41–end

			Principal Service	3rd Service	2nd Service
Thursday	**19 March** Joseph of Nazareth	W	2 Samuel 7.4–16 Psalm 89.26–36 Romans 4.13–18 Matthew 1.18–end	MP Psalms 25, 147.1–12 Isaiah 11.1–10 Matthew 13.54–end	EP Psalms 1, 112 Genesis 50.22–end Matthew 2.13–end
			Holy Communion	**Morning Prayer**	**Evening Prayer**
Friday	**20 March** Cuthbert, bishop, missionary, 687 (see p.82)	P(La)w	Hosea 14 Psalm 81.6–10, 13, 16 Mark 12.28–34	Psalm **22** or 142, **144** Exodus 1.1–14 Hebrews 7.1–end	Psalm **69** or **145** Jeremiah 15.10–end John 8.48–end
Saturday	**21 March** Thomas Cranmer, archbishop, Reformation martyr, 1556 (see p.79)	P(La)r	Hosea 5.15—6.6 Psalm 51.1–2, 17–end Luke 18.9–14	Psalm **31** or **147** Exodus 1.22—2.10 Hebrews 8	Psalms **116**, 130 or **148**, 149, 150 Jeremiah 16.10—17.4 John 9.1–17

	Principal Service	3rd Service	2nd Service
Sunday 22 March P(La) **4th Sunday of Lent**	1 Samuel 16.1–13 Psalm 23 Ephesians 5.8–14 John 9	Psalm 19 Isaiah 43.1–7 Ephesians 2.8–14	Psalm 31.1–16 [or 31.1–8] Micah 7 or Prayer of Manasseh James 5 HC John 3.14–21

For Mothering Sunday:
Exodus 2.1–10 or 1 Samuel 1.20–end; Psalm 34.11–20 or 127.1–4;
2 Corinthians 1.3–7 or Colossians 3.12–17; Luke 2.33–35 or John 19.25b–27
If the Principal Service readings have been displaced by Mothering Sunday provisions, they may be used at the Second Service.

The following readings may replace those provided for Holy Communion on any day (except the Annunciation) during the Fourth Week of Lent: Micah 7.7–9; Psalm 27.1, 9–10, 16–17; John 9

	Holy Communion	Morning Prayer	Evening Prayer
Monday 23 March P(La)	Isaiah 65.17–21 Psalm 30.1–5, 8, 11–end John 4.43–end	Psalms 70, 77 or 1, 2, 3 Exodus 2.11–22 Hebrews 9.1–14	Psalms 25, 28 or 4, 7 Jeremiah 17.5–18 John 9.18–end
Tuesday 24 March P(La) Walter Hilton, mystic, 1396 Paul Couturier, priest, ecumenist, 1953 Oscar Romero, archbishop, martyr, 1980	Ezekiel 47.1–9, 12 Psalm 46.1–8 John 5.1–3, 5–16	Psalms 54, 79 or 5, 6 (8) Exodus 2.23—3.20 Hebrews 9.15–end	**1st EP of The Annunciation** Psalm 85 Wisdom 9.1–12 or Genesis 3.8–15 Galatians 4.1–5

	Principal Service	3rd Service	2nd Service
Wednesday 25 March Gold or W **Annunciation of Our Lord to the Blessed Virgin Mary**	Isaiah 7.10–14 Psalm 40.5–11 Hebrews 10.4–10 Luke 1.26–38	MP Psalms 111, 113 1 Samuel 2.1–10 Romans 5.12–end	EP Psalms 131, 146 Isaiah 52.1–12 Hebrews 2.5–end

	Holy Communion	Morning Prayer	Evening Prayer
Thursday 26 March P(La) Harriet Monsell, founder of the Community of St John the Baptist, 1883	Exodus 32.7–14 Psalm 106.19–23 John 5.31–end	Psalms 53, 86 or 14, 15, 16 Exodus 4.27—6.1 Hebrews 10.19–25	Psalm 94 or 18* Jeremiah 19.1–13 John 10.22–end
Friday 27 March P(La)	Wisdom 2.1, 12–22 or Jeremiah 26.8–11 Psalm 34.15–end John 7.1–2, 10, 25–30	Psalm 102 or 17, 19 Exodus 6.2–13 Hebrews 10.26–end	Psalms 13, 16 or 22 Jeremiah 19.14—20.6 John 11.1–16
Saturday 28 March P(La)	Jeremiah 11.18–20 Psalm 7.1–2, 8–10 John 7.40–52	Psalm 32 or 20, 21, 23 Exodus 7.8–end Hebrews 11.1–16	Psalms 140, 141, 142 or 24, 25 Jeremiah 20.7–end John 11.17–27

Lent 5

	P(La)	Principal Service	3rd Service	2nd Service
		Holy Communion	Morning Prayer	Evening Prayer
Sunday 29 March **5th Sunday of Lent** *Passiontide begins*	P(La)	Ezekiel 37.1–14 Psalm 130 Romans 8.6–11 John 11.1–45	Psalm 86 Jeremiah 31.27–37 John 12.20–33	Psalm 30 Lamentations 3.19–33 Matthew 20.17–end

The following readings may replace those provided for Holy Communion on any day during the Fifth Week of Lent:
2 Kings 4.18–21, 32–37; Psalm 17.1–8, 16; John 11.1–45

	P(La)	Principal Service	3rd Service	2nd Service
Monday 30 March	P(La)	Susannah 1–9, 15–17, 19–30, 33–62 [or 41b–62] or Joshua 2.1–14 Psalm 23 John 8.1–11	Psalms **73**, 121 or 27, **30** Exodus 8.1–19 Hebrews 11.17–31	Psalms **26**, 27 or 26, **28**, 29 Jeremiah 21.1–10 John 11.28–44
Tuesday 31 March *John Donne, priest, poet, 1631*	P(La)	Numbers 21.4–9 Psalm 102.1–3, 16–23 John 8.21–30	Psalms **35**, 123 or 32, **36** Exodus 8.20–end Hebrews 11.32—12.2	Psalms **61**, 64 or **33** Jeremiah 22.1–5, 13–19 John 11.45–end
Wednesday 1 April *Frederick Denison Maurice, priest,* *teacher of the faith, 1872*	P(La)	Daniel 3.14–20, 24–25, 28 *Canticle:* Bless the Lord John 8.31–42	Psalms **55**, 124 or **34** Exodus 9.1–12 Hebrews 12.3–13	Psalms 56, **62** or 1**19.33–56** Jeremiah 22.20—23.8 John 12.1–11
Thursday 2 April	P(La)	Genesis 17.3–9 Psalm 105.4–9 John 8.51–end	Psalms **40**, 125 or **37*** Exodus 9.13–end Hebrews 12.14–end	Psalms 42, **43** or 39, **40** Jeremiah 23.9–32 John 12.12–19
Friday 3 April	P(La)	Jeremiah 20.10–13 Psalm 18.1–6 John 10.31–end	Psalms **22**, 126 or **31** Exodus 10 Hebrews 13.1–16	Psalm **31** or **35** Jeremiah 24 John 12.20–36a
Saturday 4 April	P(La)	Ezekiel 37.21–end *Canticle:* Jeremiah 31.10–13 or Psalm 121 John 11.45–end	Psalms **23**, 127 or 41, **42**, 43 Exodus 11 Hebrews 13.17–end	Psalms 128, 129, **130** or 45, **46** Jeremiah 25.1–14 John 12.36b–end

		Principal Service	3rd Service	2nd Service
Sunday 5 April **Palm Sunday**	R	*Liturgy of the Palms:* Matthew 21.1–11 Psalm 118.1–2,19–end [or 118.19–24] *Liturgy of the Passion:* Isaiah 50.4–9a Psalm 31.9–16 [or 31.9–18] Philippians 2.5–11 Matthew 26.14—end of 27 [or Matthew 27.11–54]	Psalms 61, 62 Zechariah 9.9–12 Luke 16.19–end	Psalm 80 Isaiah 5.1–7 Matthew 21.33–end
		Holy Communion	**Morning Prayer**	**Evening Prayer**
			From the Monday of Holy Week until the Saturday of Easter Week the seasonal psalmody must be used.	
Monday 6 April *Monday of Holy Week*	R	Isaiah 42.1–9 Psalm 36.5–11 Hebrews 9.11–15 John 12.1–11	Psalm 41 Lamentations 1.1–12a Luke 22.1–23	Psalm 25 Lamentations 2.8–19 Colossians 1.18–23
Tuesday 7 April *Tuesday of Holy Week*	R	Isaiah 49.1–7 Psalm 71.1–14 [or 71.1–8] 1 Corinthians 1.18–31 John 12.20–36	Psalm 27 Lamentations 3.1–18 Luke 22.[24–38] 39–53	Psalm 55.13–24 Lamentations 3.40–51 Galatians 6.11–end
Wednesday 8 April *Wednesday of Holy Week*	R	Isaiah 50.4–9a Psalm 70 Hebrews 12.1–3 John 13.21–32	Psalm 102 [or 102.1–18] Wisdom 1.16—2.1; 2.12–22 or Jeremiah 11.18–20 Luke 22.54–end	Psalm 88 Isaiah 63.1–9 Revelation 14.18—15.4
Thursday 9 April *Maundy Thursday*	W	Exodus 12.1–4 [5–10] 11–14 Psalm 116.1, 10–end [or 116.9–end] 1 Corinthians 11.23–26 John 13.1–17, 31b–35	Psalms 42, 43 Leviticus 16.2–24 Luke 23.1–25	Psalm 39 Exodus 11 Ephesians 2.11–18
Friday 10 April *Good Friday*	*Hangings removed;* *R for the Liturgy*	Isaiah 52.13—end of 53 Psalm 22 [or 22.1–11 or 22.1–21] Hebrews 10.16–25 or Hebrews 4.14–16; 5.7–9 John 18.1—end of 19	Psalm 69 Genesis 22.1–18 *A part of John 18 and 19 may be read, if not used at the Principal Service* or Hebrews 10.1–10	Psalms 130, 143 Lamentations 5.15–end John 19.38–end or Colossians 1.18–23

		Principal Service	3rd Service	2nd Service
Saturday	**11 April** **Easter Eve** *These readings are for use at services other than the Easter Vigil.* *Hangings removed*	Job 14.1–14 or Lamentations 3.1–9, 19–24 Psalm 31.1–4, 15–16 [or 31.1–5] 1 Peter 4.1–8 Matthew 27.57–end or John 19.38–end	Psalm 142 Hosea 6.1–6 John 2.18–22	Psalm 116 Job 19.21–27 1 John 5.5–12
		Vigil Readings	**Complementary Psalmody**	
Saturday **or Sunday**	**11 April evening** **12 April morning** *Easter Vigil* The New Testament readings should be preceded by a minimum of three Old Testament readings. The Exodus reading should always be used. *Gold or W*	Genesis 1.1—2.4a Genesis 7.1–5, 11–18; 8.6–18; 9.8–13 Genesis 22.1–18 **Exodus 14.10–end; 15.20–21** Isaiah 55.1–11 Baruch 3.9–15, 32—4.4 or Proverbs 8.1–8, 19–21; 9.4b–6 Ezekiel 36.24–28 Ezekiel 37.1–14 Zephaniah 3.14–end **Romans 6.3–11** **Matthew 28.1–10**	Psalm 136.1–9, 23–end Psalm 46 Psalm 16 *Canticle:* **Exodus 15.1b–13, 17–18** *Canticle:* Isaiah 12.2–end Psalm 19 Psalms 42, 43 Psalm 143 Psalm 98 **Psalm 114**	
		Principal Service	**3rd Service**	**2nd Service**
Sunday	**12 April** **Easter Day** *Gold or W*	Acts 10.34–43 † or Jeremiah 31.1–6 Psalm 118.1–2, 14–24 [or 118.14–24] Colossians 3.1–4 or Acts 10.34–43† John 20.1–18 or Matthew 28.1–10 † The reading from Acts must be used as either the first or second reading.	MP Psalms 114, 117 Exodus 14.10–18, 26—15.2 Revelation 15.2–4	EP Psalms 105 or 66.1–11 Song of Solomon 3.2–5; 8.6–7 John 20.11–18 *if not used at the Principal Service* or Revelation 1.12–18

		Holy Communion	Morning Prayer	Evening Prayer
Monday	**13 April** W Monday of Easter Week	Acts 2.14, 22–32 Psalm 16.1–2, 6–end Matthew 28.8–15	Psalms 111, 117, 146 Exodus 12.1–14 1 Corinthians 15.1–11	Psalm 135 Song of Solomon 1.9—2.7 Mark 16.1–8
Tuesday	**14 April** W Tuesday of Easter Week	Acts 2.36–41 Psalm 33.4–5, 18–end John 20.11–18	Psalms 112, 147.1–12 Exodus 12.14–36 1 Corinthians 15.12–19	Psalm 136 Song of Solomon 2.8–end Luke 24.1–12
Wednesday	**15 April** W Wednesday of Easter Week	Acts 3.1–10 Psalm 105.1–9 Luke 24.13–35	Psalms 113, 147.13–end Exodus 12.37–end 1 Corinthians 15.20–28	Psalm 105 Song of Solomon 3 Matthew 28.16–end
Thursday	**16 April** W Thursday of Easter Week	Acts 3.11–end Psalm 8 Luke 24.35–48	Psalms 114, 148 Exodus 13.1–16 1 Corinthians 15.29–34	Psalm 106 Song of Solomon 5.2—6.3 Luke 7.11–17
Friday	**17 April** W Friday of Easter Week	Acts 4.1–12 Psalm 118.1–4, 22–26 John 21.1–14	Psalms 115, 149 Exodus 13.17—14.14 1 Corinthians 15.35–50	Psalm 107 Song of Solomon 7.10—8.4 Luke 8.41–end
Saturday	**18 April** W Saturday of Easter Week	Acts 4.13–21 Psalm 118.1–4, 14–21 Mark 16.9–15	Psalms 116, 150 Exodus 14.15–end 1 Corinthians 15.51–end	Psalm 145 Song of Solomon 8.5–7 John 11.17–44

Easter 2

		Principal Service	3rd Service	2nd Service
Sunday 19 April W	**2nd Sunday of Easter**	[Exodus 14.10-end; 15.20-21] / Acts 2.14a, 22-32 † / Psalm 16 / 1 Peter 1.3-9 / John 20.19-end / † *The reading from Acts must be used as either the first or second reading.*	Psalm 81.1-10 / Exodus 12.1-17 / 1 Corinthians 5.6b-8	Psalm 30.1-5 / Daniel 6.1-23 or 6.6-23 / Mark 15.46—16.8

		Holy Communion	Morning Prayer	Evening Prayer
Monday 20 April W		Acts 4.23-31 / Psalm 2.1-9 / John 3.1-8	Psalm 2, 19 or 1, 2, 3 / Exodus 15.1-21 / Colossians 1.1-14	Psalm 139 or 4, 7 / Deuteronomy 1.3-18 / John 20.1-10
Tuesday 21 April W	Anselm, abbot, archbishop, teacher of the faith, 1109 (see p.80)	Acts 4.32-end / Psalm 93 / John 3.7-15	Psalms 8, 20, 21 or 5, 6 (8) / Exodus 15.22—16.10 / Colossians 1.15-end	Psalm 104 or 9, 10* / Deuteronomy 1.19-40 / John 20.11-18
Wednesday 22 April W		Acts 5.17-26 / Psalm 34.1-8 / John 3.16-21	Psalms 16, **30** or 119.1-32 / Exodus 16.11-end / Colossians 2.1-15	Psalm 33 or 11, 12, 13 / Deuteronomy 3.18-end / John 20.19-end

or: 1st EP of George, martyr, patron of England:
Psalms 111, 116; Jeremiah 15.15-21; Hebrews 11.32—12.2

		Principal Service	3rd Service	2nd Service
Thursday 23 April R	George, martyr, patron of England, c.304	1 Maccabees 2.59-64 or Revelation 12.7-12 / Psalm 126 / 2 Timothy 2.3-13 / John 15.18-21	MP Psalms 5, 146 / Joshua 1.1-9 / Ephesians 6.10-20	EP Psalms 3, 11 / Isaiah 43.1-7 / John 15.1-8

		Holy Communion	Morning Prayer	Evening Prayer
Friday 24 April W	Mellitus, bishop, 624 / Seven Martyrs of the Melanesian Brotherhood, 2003	Acts 5.34-42 / Psalm 27.1-5, 16-17 / John 6.1-15	Psalms 57, **61** or 17, **19** / Exodus 18.1-12 / Colossians 3.12—4.1	Psalm 118 or **22** / Deuteronomy 4.15-31 / John 21.1-14 / or: 1st EP of Mark the Evangelist: Psalm 19; Isaiah 52.7-10; Mark 1.1-15

		Principal Service	3rd Service	2nd Service
Saturday 25 April R	Mark the Evangelist	Proverbs 15.28-end or Acts 15.35-end / Psalm 119.9-16 / Ephesians 4.7-16 / Mark 13.5-13	MP Psalms 37.23-end, 148 / Isaiah 62.6-10 or Ecclesiasticus 51.13-end / Acts 12.25—13.13	EP Psalm 45 / Ezekiel 1.4-14 / 2 Timothy 4.1-11

Easter 3

	Principal Service	3rd Service	2nd Service
Sunday 26 April **3rd Sunday of Easter** W	[Zephaniah 3.14–end] Acts 2.14a, 36–41 † Psalm 116.1–3, 10–end [or 116.1–7] 1 Peter 1.17–23 Luke 24.13–35 † The reading from Acts must be used as either the first or second reading.	Psalm 23 Isaiah 40.1–11 1 Peter 5.1–11	Psalm 48 Haggai 1.13—2.9 1 Corinthians 3.10–17 HC John 2.13–22

	Holy Communion	Morning Prayer	Evening Prayer
Monday 27 April *Christina Rossetti, poet, 1894* W	Acts 6.8–15 Psalm 119.17–24 John 6.22–29	Psalms 96, 97 or 27, 30 Exodus 19 Luke 1.1–25	Psalm 61, 65 or 26, 28, 29 Deuteronomy 5.1–22 Ephesians 1.1–14
Tuesday 28 April *Peter Chanel, missionary, martyr, 1841* W	Acts 7.51—8.1a Psalm 31.1–5, 16 John 6.30–35	Psalms 98, 99, 100 or 32, 36 Exodus 20.1–21 Luke 1.26–38	Psalm 71 or 33 Deuteronomy 5.22–end Ephesians 1.15–end
Wednesday 29 April *Catherine of Siena,* *teacher of the faith, 1380 (see p.80)* W	Acts 8.1b–8 Psalm 66.1–6 John 6.35–40	Psalm 105 or 34 Exodus 24 Luke 1.39–56	Psalms 67, 72 or 119.33–56 Deuteronomy 6 Ephesians 2.1–10
Thursday 30 April *Pandita Mary Ramabai, translator, 1922* W	Acts 8.26–end Psalm 66.7–8, 14–end John 6.44–51	Psalm 136 or 37* Exodus 25.1–22 Luke 1.57–end	Psalm 73 or 39, 40 Deuteronomy 7.1–11 Ephesians 2.11–end or: 1st EP of Philip and James, Apostles: Psalm 25; Isaiah 40.27–end; John 12.20–26

	Principal Service	3rd Service	2nd Service
Friday 1 May Philip and James, Apostles R	Isaiah 30.15–21 Psalm 119.1–8 Ephesians 1.3–10 John 14.1–14	MP Psalms 139, 146 Proverbs 4.10–18 James 1.1–12	EP Psalm 149 Job 23.1–12 John 1.43–end

	Holy Communion	Morning Prayer	Evening Prayer
Saturday 2 May *Athanasius, bishop,* *teacher of the faith, 373 (see p.80)* W	Acts 9.31–42 Psalm 116.10–15 John 6.60–69	Psalms 108, 110, 111 or 41, 42, 43 Exodus 29.1–9 Luke 2.21–40	Psalms 23, 27 or 45, 46 Deuteronomy 8 Ephesians 3.14–end

		Principal Service	3rd Service	2nd Service
Sunday 3 May **4th Sunday of Easter**	W	[Genesis 7] Acts 2.42–end † Psalm 23 1 Peter 2.19–end John 10.1–10 † *The reading from Acts must be used as either the first or second reading.*	Psalm 106.6–24 Nehemiah 9.6–15 1 Corinthians 10.1–13	Psalm 29.1–10 Ezra 3.1–13 Ephesians 2.11–end *HC* Luke 19.37–end
		Holy Communion	**Morning Prayer**	**Evening Prayer**
Monday 4 May English saints and martyrs of the Reformation Era	W	Acts 11.1–18 Psalms 42.1–2; 43.1–4 John 10.1–10 (or 11–18) *Lesser Festival eucharistic lectionary:* Isaiah 43.1–7 or Ecclesiasticus 2.10–17 Psalm 87 2 Corinthians 4.5–12 John 12.20–26	Psalm **103** or **44** Exodus 32.1–14 Luke 2.41–end	Psalms 112, 113, **114** or **47**, 49 Deuteronomy 9.1–21 Ephesians 4.1–16
Tuesday 5 May	W	Acts 11.19–26 Psalm 87 John 10.22–30	Psalm **139**, or **48** 52 Exodus 32.15–34 Luke 3.1–14	Psalms 115, **116** or **50** Deuteronomy 9.23—10.5 Ephesians 4.17–end
Wednesday 6 May	W	Acts 12.24—13.5 Psalm 67 John 12.44–end	Psalm **135**, or 119.**57–80** Exodus 33 Luke 3.15–22	Psalms **47**, 48 or **59**, 60 (67) Deuteronomy 10.12–end Ephesians 5.1–14
Thursday 7 May	W	Acts 13.13–25 Psalm 89.1–2, 20–26 John 13.16–20	Psalm **118** or 56, **57** (63*) Exodus 34.1–10, 27–end Luke 4.1–13	Psalm 81, **85** or 61, **62**, 64 Deuteronomy 11.8–end Ephesians 5.15–end
Friday 8 May Julian of Norwich, spiritual writer, c.1417 (see p.82)	W	Acts 13.26–33 Psalm 2 John 14.1–6	Psalm **33** or **51**, 54 Exodus 35.20—36.7 Luke 4.14–30	Psalms 36, 40 or **38** Deuteronomy 12.1–14 Ephesians 6.1–9
Saturday 9 May	W	Acts 13.44–end Psalm 98.1–5 John 14.7–14	Psalm **34** or **68** Exodus 40.17–end Luke 4.31–37	Psalms **84**, 86 or 65, **66** Deuteronomy 15.1–18 Ephesians 6.10–end

		Principal Service	3rd Service	2nd Service
Sunday 10 May 5th Sunday of Easter	W	[Genesis 8.1–19] Acts 7.55–end † Psalm 31.1–5, 15–16 [or 31.1–5] 1 Peter 2.2–10 John 14.1–14 † The reading from Acts must be used as either the first or second reading.	Psalm 30 Ezekiel 37.1–12 John 5.19–29	Psalm 147.1–12 Zechariah 4.1–10 Revelation 21.1–14 HC Luke 2.25–32 [33–38]
		Holy Communion	**Morning Prayer**	**Evening Prayer**
Monday 11 May	W	Acts 14.5–18 Psalm 118.1–3, 14–15 John 14.21–26	Psalm **145** or **71** Numbers 9.15–end; 10.33–end Luke 4.38–end	Psalm **105** or **72**, 75 Deuteronomy 16.1–20 1 Peter 1.1–12
Tuesday 12 May *Gregory Dix, priest, monk, scholar, 1952*	W	Acts 14.19–end Psalm 145.10–end John 14.27–end	Psalms 19, 147.1–12 or **73** Numbers 11.1–33 Luke 5.1–11	Psalms 96, **97** or **74** Deuteronomy 17.8–end 1 Peter 1.13–end
Wednesday 13 May	W	Acts 15.1–6 Psalm 122.1–5 John 15.1–8	Psalms **30**, 147.13–end or **77** Numbers 12 Luke 5.12–26	Psalms 98, **99**, 100 or 119.81–104 Deuteronomy 18.9–end 1 Peter 2.1–10 *or:* 1st EP of Matthias the Apostle: Psalm 147; Isaiah 22.15–22; Philippians 3.13b—4.1
		Principal Service	**3rd Service**	**2nd Service**
Thursday 14 May *Matthias the Apostle*	R	Isaiah 22.15–end or Acts 1.15–end Psalm 15 Acts 1.15–end or 1 Corinthians 4.1–7 John 15.9–17	MP Psalms 16, 147.1–12 1 Samuel 2.27–35 Acts 2.37–end	EP Psalm 80 1 Samuel 16.1–13a Matthew 7.15–27
		Holy Communion	**Morning Prayer**	**Evening Prayer**
Friday 15 May	W	Acts 15.22–31 Psalm 57.8–end John 15.12–17	Psalms **138**, 149 or **55** Numbers 14.1–25 Luke 6.1–11	Psalm **66** or **69** Deuteronomy 21.22—22.8 1 Peter 3.1–12
Saturday 16 May *Caroline Chisholm, social reformer, 1877*	W	Acts 16.1–10 Psalm 100 John 15.18–21	Psalms **146**, 150 or **76**, 79 Numbers 14.26–end Luke 6.12–26	Psalm 118 or 81, **84** Deuteronomy 24.5–end 1 Peter 3.13–end

		Principal Service	3rd Service	2nd Service
Sunday	**17 May** W **6th Sunday of Easter**	[Genesis 8.20—9.17] Acts 17.22-31 † Psalm 66.7-end 1 Peter 3.13-end John 14.15-21 † *The reading from Acts must be used as either the first or second reading.*	Psalm 73.21-28 Job 14.1-2, 7-15; 19.23-27a 1 Thessalonians 4.13-end	Psalms 87, 36.5-10 Zechariah 8.1-13 Revelation 21.22—22.5 HC John 21.1-14

		Holy Communion	Morning Prayer	Evening Prayer
Monday	**18 May** W Rogation Day	Acts 16.11-15 Psalm 149.1-5 John 15.26—16.4	Psalms **65**, 67 or 80, **82** Numbers 16.1-35 Luke 6.27-38	Psalms **121**, 122, 123 or **85**, 86 Deuteronomy 26 1 Peter 4.1-11
Tuesday	**19 May** W Rogation Day Dunstan, archbishop, monastic reformer, 988 (see p.81)	Acts 16.22-34 Psalm 138 John 16.5-11	Psalms 124, 125, **126**, 127 or 87, **89.1-18** Numbers 16.36-end Luke 6.39-end	Psalms **128**, 129, 130, 131 or **89.19-end** Deuteronomy 28.1-14 1 Peter 4.12-end
Wednesday	**20 May** W Rogation Day Alcuin, deacon, abbot, 804 (see p.82)	Acts 17.15, 22—18.1 Psalm 148.1-2, 11-end John 16.12-15	Psalms **132**, 133 or **119.105-128** Numbers 17.1-11 Luke 7.1-10	1st EP of Ascension Day Psalms 15, 24 2 Samuel 23.1-5 Colossians 2.20—3.4

Ascension Day

	Principal Service	3rd Service	2nd Service
Thursday 21 May Ascension Day *Gold or W*	Acts 1.1–11 † or Daniel 7.9–14 Psalm 47 or Psalm 93 Ephesians 1.15–end or Acts 1.1–11 † Luke 24.44–end † *The reading from Acts must be used as either the first or second reading.*	MP Psalms 110, 150 Isaiah 52.7–end Hebrews 7.[11–25] 26–end	EP Psalm 8 Song of the Three 29–37 or 2 Kings 2.1–15 Revelation 5 HC Mark 16.14–end

The nine days after Ascension Day until the eve of Pentecost are observed as days of prayer and preparation for the celebration of the outpouring of the Holy Spirit.
From 22–30 May, in preparation for the Day of Pentecost, an alternative sequence of daily readings for use at the one of the offices is marked with an asterisk *.*

	Holy Communion	Morning Prayer	Evening Prayer
Friday 22 May W	Acts 18.9–18 Psalm 47.1–6 John 16.20–23	Psalms 20, 81 or 88 (95) Numbers 20.1–13 Luke 7.11–17 * Exodus 35.30—36.1; *Galatians 5.13–end*	Psalm 145 or 102 Deuteronomy 29.2–15 1 John 1.1—2.6
Saturday 23 May W	Acts 18.22–end Psalm 47.1–2, 7–end John 16.23–28	Psalms 21, 47 or 96, 97, 100 Numbers 21.4–9 Luke 7.18–35 *Numbers 11.16–17, 24–29; 1 Corinthians 2*	Psalms 84, 85 or 104 Deuteronomy 30 1 John 2.7–17

Easter 7

		Principal Service	3rd Service	2nd Service
Sunday	W	[Ezekiel 36.24–28]	Psalm 104.26–35	Psalm 47
24 May		Acts 1.6–14 †	Isaiah 65.17–end	2 Samuel 23.1–5
7th Sunday of Easter		Psalm 68.1–10, 32–end [or 68.1–10]	Revelation 21.1–8	Ephesians 1.15–end
Sunday after Ascension Day		1 Peter 4.12–14; 5.6–11		HC Mark 16.14–end
		John 17.1–11		
		† *The reading from Acts must be used as either the first or second reading.*		

		Holy Communion	Morning Prayer	Evening Prayer
Monday	W	Acts 19.1–8	Psalms 93, 96, 97 or **98**, 99, 101	Psalm **18** or **105*** (or 103)
25 May		Psalm 68.1–6	Numbers 22.1–35	Deuteronomy 31.1–13
The Venerable Bede, monk,		John 16.29–end	Luke 7.36–end	1 John 2.18–end
scholar, historian, 735 (see p.82);			*Numbers 27.15–end; 1 Corinthians 3	
Aldhelm, bishop, 709				
Tuesday	W	Acts 20.17–27	Psalms 98, **99**, 100 or **106*** (or 103)	Psalm **68** or **107***
26 May		Psalm 68.9–10, 18–19	Numbers 22.36–23.12	Deuteronomy 31.14–29
Augustine, archbishop, 605 (see p.81);		John 17.1–11	Luke 8.1–15	1 John 3.1–10
John Calvin, reformer, 1564;			*1 Samuel 10.1–10; 1 Corinthians 12.1–13	
Philip Neri, founder of the Oratorians,				
spiritual guide, 1595				
Wednesday	W	Acts 20.28–end	Psalms 2, **29** or 110, **111**, 112	Psalms 36, **46** or **119.129–152**
27 May		Psalm 68.27–28, 32–end	Numbers 23.13–end	Deuteronomy 31.30—32.14
		John 17.11–19	Luke 8.16–25	1 John 3.11–end
			*1 Kings 19.1–18; Matthew 3.13–end	
Thursday	W	Acts 22.30, 23.6–11	Psalms **24**.72 or 113, **115**	Psalm **139** or 114, **116**, 117
28 May		Psalm 16.1, 5–end	Numbers 24	Deuteronomy 32.15–47
Lanfranc, monk, archbishop, scholar, 1089		John 17.20–end	Luke 8.26–39	1 John 4.1–6
			*Ezekiel 11.14–20; Matthew 9.35—10.20	
Friday	W	Acts 25.13–21	Psalms **28**, 30 or **139**	Psalm **147** or **130**, 131, 137
29 May		Psalm 103.1–2, 11–12, 19–20	Numbers 27.12–end	Deuteronomy 33
		John 21.15–19	Luke 8.40–end	1 John 4.7–end
			*Ezekiel 36.22–28; Matthew 12.22–32	
Saturday	W	Acts 28.16–20, 30–end	Psalms 42, **43** or 120, **121**, 122	**1st EP of Pentecost**
30 May		Psalm 11.4–end	Numbers 32.1–27	Psalm 48
Josephine Butler, social reformer, 1906		John 21.20–end	Luke 9.1–17	Deuteronomy 16.9–15
(see p.83)			*Micah 3.1–8; Ephesians 6.10–20 (at MP only)	John 15.26—16.5
Joan of Arc, visionary, 1431				
Apolo Kivebulaya, priest, evangelist, 1933				

		Principal Service	3rd Service	2nd Service
Sunday	**31 May** R **Pentecost** *Whit Sunday*	Acts 2.1–21 † or Numbers 11.24–30 Psalm 104.26–36, 37b [or 104.26–end] 1 Corinthians 12.3b–13 or Acts 2.1–21 † John 20.19–23 or John 7.37–39 † *The reading from Acts must be used as either the first or second reading.*	MP Psalm 87 Genesis 11.1–9 Acts 10.34–48	EP Psalms 67, 133 Joel 2.21–end Acts 2.14–21 [22–38] HC Luke 24.44–end
Monday	**1 June** W Visit of the Blessed Virgin Mary to Elizabeth *(transferred from 31 May)* Ordinary Time resumes today	Zephaniah 3.14–18 Psalm 113 Romans 12.9–16 Luke 1.39–49 [50–56]	MP Psalms 85, 150 1 Samuel 2.1–10 Mark 3.31–end	EP Psalms 122, 127, 128 Zechariah 2.10–end John 3.25–30
		Holy Communion	Morning Prayer	Evening Prayer
Tuesday	**2 June** G DEL week 9	2 Peter 3.11–15a, 17–end Psalm 90.1–4, 10, 14, 16 Mark 12.13–17	Psalms **132**, 133 Joshua 2 Luke 9.28–36	Psalms (134), **135** Job 2 Romans 1.18–end
Wednesday	**3 June** G *Martyrs of Uganda, 1885–7, 1977*	2 Timothy 1.1–3, 6–12 Psalm 123 Mark 12.18–27	Psalm 119.**153–end** Joshua 3 Luke 9.37–50	Psalm **136** Job 3 Romans 2.1–16
Thursday	**4 June** G *Petroc, abbot, 6th cent.*	2 Timothy 2.8–15 Psalm 25.4–12 Mark 12.28–34	Psalms **143**, 146 Joshua 4.1—5.1 Luke 9.51–end	Psalms **138**, 140, 141 Job 4 Romans 2.17–end
Friday	**5 June** Gr Boniface (Wynfrith), bishop, martyr, 754 (see p.79)	2 Timothy 3.10–end Psalm 119.161–168 Mark 12.35–37	Psalms 142, **144** Joshua 5.2–end Luke 10.1–16	Psalm **145** Job 5 Romans 3.1–20
Saturday	**6 June** G *Ini Kopuria, founder of* *the Melanesian Brotherhood, 1945*	2 Timothy 4.1–8 Psalm 71.7–16 Mark 12.38–end	Psalm **147** Joshua 6.1–20 Luke 10.17–24	**1st EP of Trinity Sunday** Psalms 97, 98 Exodus 34.1–10 Mark 1.1–13

			Principal Service	3rd Service	2nd Service
Sunday	**7 June** Trinity Sunday	*Gold or* W	Isaiah 40.12–17, 27–end Psalm 8 2 Corinthians 13.11–end Matthew 28.16–20	*MP* Psalm 86.8–13 Exodus 3.1–6, 13–15 John 17.1–11	*EP* Psalms 93, 150 Isaiah 6.1–8 John 16.5–15
			Holy Communion	**Morning Prayer**	**Evening Prayer**
Monday	**8 June** Thomas Ken, bishop, nonjuror, hymn writer, 1711 (see p.81) DEL week 10	*Gw*	1 Kings 17.1–6 Psalm 121 Matthew 5.1–12	Psalms **1**, 2, 3 Joshua 7.1–15 Luke 10.25–37	Psalms **4**, 7 Job 7 Romans 4.1–12
Tuesday	**9 June** Columba, abbot, missionary, 597 (see p.82) *Ephrem, deacon, hymn writer,* *teacher of the faith, 373*	*Gw*	1 Kings 17.7–16 Psalm 4 Matthew 5.13–16	Psalms **5**, 6 (8) Joshua 7.16–end Luke 10.38–end	Psalms **9**, 10* Job 8 Romans 4.13–end

Trinity Sunday

If Corpus Christi is kept as a Festival:

			Holy Communion	Morning Prayer	Evening Prayer
Wednesday	10 June	G	1 Kings 18.20–39 Psalm 16.1, 6–end Matthew 5.17–19	Psalm 119.1–32 Joshua 8.1–29 Luke 11.1–13	Psalms 11, 12, 13 Job 9 Romans 5.1–11 *or:* 1st EP of Corpus Christi: Psalms 110, 111; Exodus 16.2–15; John 6.22–35
			Principal Service	**3rd Service**	**2nd Service**
Thursday	**11 June** Day of Thanksgiving for the Institution of Holy Communion (Corpus Christi)	W	Genesis 14.18–20 Psalm 116.10–end 1 Corinthians 11.23–26 John 6.51–58	MP Psalm 147 Deuteronomy 8.2–16 1 Corinthians 10.1–17	EP Psalms 23, 42, 43 Proverbs 9.1–5 Luke 9.11–17
Friday	**12 June** Barnabas the Apostle *(transferred from 11 June)*	R	Job 29.11–16 *or* Acts 11.19–end Psalm 112 Acts 11.19–end *or* Galatians 2.1–10 John 15.12–17	MP Psalms 100, 101, 117 Jeremiah 9.23–24 Acts 4.32–end	EP Psalm 147 Ecclesiastes 12.9–end *or* Tobit 4.5–11 Acts 9.26–31
			Holy Communion	**Morning Prayer**	
Saturday	13 June	G	1 Kings 19.19–end Psalm 16.1–7 Matthew 5.33–37	Psalms 20, 21, 23 Joshua 10.1–15 Luke 11.37–end	Psalms 24, 25 Job 12 Romans 6.15–end

Trinity Sunday

If Corpus Christi is not kept as a Festival:

		Holy Communion	Morning Prayer	Evening Prayer
Wednesday 10 June	G	1 Kings 18.20–39 Psalm 16.1, 6–end Matthew 5.17–19	Psalm 119.1–32 Joshua 8.1–29 Luke 11.1–13	Psalms 11, 12, 13 Job 9 Romans 5.1–11 *or:* 1st EP of Barnabas the Apostle: Psalms 1, 15; Isaiah 42.5–12; Acts 14.8–end
		Principal Service	3rd Service	2nd Service
Thursday 11 June Barnabas the Apostle	R	Job 29.11–16 or Acts 11.19–end Psalm 112 Acts 11.19–end or Galatians 2.1–10 John 15.12–17	MP Psalms 100, 101, 117 Jeremiah 9.23–24 Acts 4.32–end	EP Psalm 147 Ecclesiastes 12.9–end or Tobit 4.5–11 Acts 9.26–31
		Holy Communion	Morning Prayer	Evening Prayer
Friday 12 June	G	1 Kings 19.9, 11–16 Psalm 27.8–16 Matthew 5.27–32	Psalms 17, 19 Joshua 9.3–26 Luke 11.29–36	Psalm 22 Job 11 Romans 6.1–14
Saturday 13 June	G	1 Kings 19.19–end Psalm 16.1–7 Matthew 5.33–37	Psalms 20, 21, 23 Joshua 24.29–end Luke 11.37–end	Psalms 24, 25 Job 12 Romans 6.15–end

		Principal Service		3rd Service	2nd Service
Sunday	**14 June** **1st Sunday after Trinity** Proper 6	G	*Continuous:* Genesis 18.1–15 [21.1–7] Psalm 116.1, 10–17 [or 116.9–17] Romans 5.1–8 Matthew 9.35—10.8 [9–23]	*Related:* Exodus 19.2–8a Psalm 100	Psalm 45 Deuteronomy 10.12—11.1 Acts 23.12–end	Psalms [42] 43 1 Samuel 21.1–15 Luke 11.14–28

		Holy Communion	Morning Prayer	Evening Prayer
Monday	**15 June** *Evelyn Underhill, spiritual writer, 1941* DEL week 11	G	1 Kings 21.1–16 Psalm 5.1–5 Matthew 5.38–42	Psalms 27, **30** Joshua 14 Luke 12.1–12	Psalms 26, **28**, 29 Job 13 Romans 7.1–6
Tuesday	**16 June** *Richard, bishop, 1253 (see p.81)* *Joseph Butler, bishop, philosopher, 1752*	Gw	1 Kings 21.17–end Psalm 51.1–9 Matthew 5.43–end	Psalms 32, **36** Joshua 21.43—22.8 Luke 12.13–21	Psalm **33** Job 14 Romans 7.7–end
Wednesday	**17 June** *Samuel and Henrietta Barnett,* *social reformers, 1913 and 1936*	G	2 Kings 2.1, 6–14 Psalm 31.21–end Matthew 6.1–6, 16–18	Psalm **34** Joshua 22.9–end Luke 12.22–31	Psalm 1**19.33–56** Job 15 Romans 8.1–11
Thursday	**18 June** *Bernard Mizeki, martyr, 1896*	G	Ecclesiasticus 48.1–14 or Isaiah 63.7–9 Psalm 97.1–8 Matthew 6.7–15	Psalm **37*** Joshua 23 Luke 12.32–40	Psalms 39, **40** Job 16.1—17.2 Romans 8.12–17
Friday	**19 June** *Sundar Singh, sadhu (holy man),* *evangelist, teacher of the faith, 1929*	G	2 Kings 11.1–4, 9–18, 20 Psalm 132.1–5, 11–13 Matthew 6.19–23	Psalm 31 Joshua 24.1–28 Luke 12.41–48	Psalm **35** Job 17.3–end Romans 8.18–30
Saturday	**20 June**	G	2 Chronicles 24.17–25 Psalm 89.25–33 Matthew 6.24–end	Psalms 41, **42**, 43 Joshua 24.29–end Luke 12.49–end	Psalms 45, **46** Job 18 Romans 8.31–end

Day		3rd Service / Morning Prayer	Principal Service / Holy Communion	2nd Service / Evening Prayer
Sunday	**21 June** G **2nd Sunday after Trinity** Proper 7	**3rd Service** Psalm 49 Deuteronomy 11.1–15 Acts 27.1–12	**Principal Service** *Continuous:* Genesis 21.8–21 Psalm 86.1–10, 16–end [or 86.1–10] / *Related:* Jeremiah 20.7–13 Psalm 69.8–11 [12–17] 18–20 [or 69.14–20] Romans 6.1b–11 Matthew 10.24–39	**2nd Service** Psalms 46 [48] 1 Samuel 24.1–17 Luke 14.12–24
Monday	**22 June** Gr Alban, first martyr of Britain, c.250 (see p.79) DEL week 12	**Morning Prayer** Psalm 44 Judges 2 Luke 13.1–9	**Holy Communion** 2 Kings 17.5–8, 13–15, 18 Psalm 60.1–5, 11–end Matthew 7.1–5	**Evening Prayer** Psalms **47**, 49 Job 19 Romans 9.1–18
Tuesday	**23 June** Gw Etheldreda, abbess, c.678 (see p.82)	Psalms **48**, 52 Judges 4.1–23 Luke 13.10–21	2 Kings 19.9b–11, 14–21, 31–36 Psalm **48**.1–2, 8–end Matthew 7.6, 12–14	Psalm **50** Job 21 Romans 9.19–end *or:* 1st EP of the Birth of John the Baptist: Psalm 71; Judges 13.2–7, 24–end; Luke 1.5–25
Wednesday	**24 June** W Birth of John the Baptist Ember Day	**3rd Service** MP Psalms 50, 149 Ecclesiasticus 48.1–10 or Malachi 3.1–6 Luke 3.1–17	**Principal Service** Isaiah 40.1–11 Psalm 85.7–end Acts 3.14b–26 or Galatians 3.23–end Luke 1.57–66, 80	**2nd Service** EP Psalms 80, 82 Malachi 4 Matthew 11.2–19
Thursday	**25 June** G	**Morning Prayer** Psalms 56, **57** (63*) Judges 6.1–24 Luke 14.1–11	**Holy Communion** 2 Kings 24.8–17 Psalm 79.1–9, 12 Matthew 7.21–end	**Evening Prayer** Psalms 61, **62**, 64 Job 23 Romans 10.11–end
Friday	**26 June** G Ember Day	Psalms **51**, 54 Judges 6.25–end Luke 14.12–24	2 Kings 25.1–12 Psalm 137.1–6 Matthew 8.1–4	Psalm **38** Job 24 Romans 11.1–12
Saturday	**27 June** G Cyril, bishop, teacher of the faith, 444 Ember Day	Psalm **68** Judges 7 Luke 14.25–end	Lamentations 2.2, 10–14, 18–19 Psalm 74.1–3, 21–end Matthew 8.5–17	Psalms 65, **66** Job 25–26 Romans 11.13–24

Trinity 3

	Principal Service	3rd Service	2nd Service
Sunday 28 June G **3rd Sunday after Trinity** Proper 8	*Continuous:* Genesis 22.1–14 Psalm 13 *Related:* Jeremiah 28.5–9 Psalm 89.1–4, 15–18 [or 89.8–18] Romans 6.12–end Matthew 10.40–end	Psalms 52, 53 Deuteronomy 15.1–11 Acts 27.[13–32] 33–end or: 1st EP of Peter and Paul, Apostles [or †Peter the Apostle alone]: Psalms 66, 67; Ezekiel 3.4–11; Galatians 1.13—2.8 [†Acts 9.32–end]	Psalm 50 [or 50.1–15] 1 Samuel 28.3–19 Luke 17.20–end
Monday 29 June R Peter and Paul, Apostles or Peter the Apostle R	*Peter and Paul:* Zechariah 4.1–6a, 10b–end or Acts 12.1–11 Psalm 125 Acts 12.1–11 or 2 Timothy 4.6–8, 17–18 Matthew 16.13–19 *Peter alone:* Ezekiel 3.22–end or Acts 12.1–11 Acts 11.1–18 Acts 12.1–11 or 1 Peter 2.19–end Matthew 16.13–19	MP Psalms 71, 113 Isaiah 49.1–6 John 21.15–22	EP Psalms 124, 138 Ezekiel 34.11–16 Psalm 125

	Holy Communion	Morning Prayer	Evening Prayer
Tuesday 30 June G DEL week 13	Amos 3.1–8, 4.11–12 Psalm 5.8–end Matthew 8.23–27	Psalm 73 Judges 9.1–21 Luke 15.11–end	Psalm 74 Job 28 Romans 12.1–8
Wednesday 1 July G *Henry, John, and Henry Venn, priests,* *evangelical divines, 1797, 1813, 1873*	Amos 5.14–15, 21–24 Psalm 50.7–14 Matthew 8.28–end	Psalm 77 Judges 9.22–end Luke 16.1–18	Psalm 119.81–104 Job 29 Romans 12.9–end
Thursday 2 July G	Amos 7.10–end Psalm 19.7–10 Matthew 9.1–8	Psalm 78.1–39* Judges 11.1–11 Luke 16.19–end	Psalm 78.40–end* Job 30 Romans 13.1–7 or: 1st EP of Thomas the Apostle: Psalm 27; Isaiah 35; Hebrews 10.35—11.1

	Principal Service	3rd Service	2nd Service
Friday 3 July R Thomas the Apostle	Habakkuk 2.1–4 Psalm 31.1–6 Ephesians 2.19–end John 20.24–29	MP Psalms 92, 146 2 Samuel 15.17–21 or Ecclesiasticus 2 John 11.1–16	EP Psalm 139 Job 42.1–6 1 Peter 1.3–12

	Holy Communion	Morning Prayer	Evening Prayer
Saturday 4 July G	Amos 9.11–end Psalm 85.8–end Matthew 9.14–17	Psalms 76, 79 Judges 12.1–7 Luke 17.11–19	Psalms 81, 84 Job 32 Romans 14.1–12

Trinity 4

		Principal Service		Holy Communion	3rd Service — Morning Prayer	2nd Service — Evening Prayer
Sunday	**5 July** **4th Sunday after Trinity** *Proper 9*	G	*Continuous:* Genesis 24.34–38, 42–49, 58–end Psalm 45.10–end or *Canticle:* Song of Solomon 2.8–13 Romans 7.15–25a Matthew 11.16–19, 25–end	*Related:* Zechariah 9.9–12 Psalm 145.8–15	Psalm 55.1–15, 18–22 Deuteronomy 24.10–end Acts 28.1–16	Psalms 56 [57] 2 Samuel 2.1–11; 3.1 Luke 18.31—19.10
Monday	**6 July** *Thomas More, scholar,* *and John Fisher, bishop,* *martyrs, 1535* DEL week 14	G	Hosea 2.14–16, 19–20 Psalm 145.2–9 Matthew 9.18–26		Psalms 80, 82 Judges 13.1–24 Luke 17.20–end	Psalms 85, 86 Job 33 Romans 14.13–end
Tuesday	**7 July**	G	Hosea 8.4–7, 11–13 Psalm 103.8–12 Matthew 9.32–end		Psalms 87, **89.1–18** Judges 14 Luke 18.1–14	Psalm **89.19–end** Job 38 Romans 15.1–13
Wednesday	**8 July**	G	Hosea 10.1–3, 7–8, 12 Psalm 115.3–10 Matthew 10.1–7		Psalms **119.105–128** Judges 15.1–16.3 Luke 18.15–30	Psalms **91**, 93 Job 39 Romans 15.14–21
Thursday	**9 July**	G	Hosea 11.1, 3–4, 8–9 Psalm 105.1–7 Matthew 10.7–15		Psalms 90, **92** Judges 16.4–end Luke 18.31–end	Psalm **94** Job 40 Romans 15.22–end
Friday	**10 July**	G	Hosea 14.2–end Psalm 80.1–7 Matthew 10.16–23		Psalms **88** (95) Judges 17 Luke 19.1–10	Psalm **102** Job 41 Romans 16.1–16
Saturday	**11 July** *Benedict, abbot, c.550 (see p.82)*	Gw	Isaiah 6.1–8 Psalm 51.1–7 Matthew 10.24–33		Psalms 96, **97**, 100 Judges 18.1–20, 27–end Luke 19.11–27	Psalm **104** Job 42 Romans 16.17–end

		Principal Service	3rd Service	2nd Service
Sunday	**12 July** **5th Sunday after Trinity** Proper 10 G	*Continuous:* Genesis 25.19–end Psalm 119.105–112 Romans 8.1–11 Matthew 13.1–9, 18–23 *Related:* Isaiah 55.10–13 Psalm 65 (or 65.8–end)	Psalms 64, 65 Deuteronomy 28.1–14 Acts 28.17–end	Psalms 60 [63] 2 Samuel 7.18–end Luke 19.41—20.8
		Holy Communion	Morning Prayer	Evening Prayer
Monday	**13 July** DEL week 15 G	Isaiah 1.11–17 Psalm 50.7–15 Matthew 10.34—11.1	Psalms **98, 99**, 101 1 Samuel 1.1–20 Luke 19.28–40	Psalms **105*** (or 103) Ezekiel 1.1–14 2 Corinthians 1.1–14
Tuesday	**14 July** John Keble, priest, poet, 1866 (see p.81) Gw	Isaiah 7.1–9 Psalm 48.1–7 Matthew 11.20–24	Psalm **106*** (or 103) 1 Samuel 1.21—2.11 Luke 19.41–end	Psalms **107*** Ezekiel 1.15—2.2 2 Corinthians 1.15—2.4
Wednesday	**15 July** Swithun, bishop, c.862 (see p.81) Bonaventure, friar, bishop, teacher of the faith, 1274 Gw	Isaiah 10.5–7, 13–16 Psalm 94.5–11 Matthew 11.25–27	Psalms 110, **111**, 112 1 Samuel 2.12–26 Luke 20.1–8	Psalm 119.**129–152** Ezekiel 2.3—3.11 2 Corinthians 2.5–end
Thursday	**16 July** Osmund, bishop, 1099 G	Isaiah 26.7–9, 16–19 Psalm 102.14–21 Matthew 11.28–end	Psalms 113, **115** 1 Samuel 2.27–end Luke 20.9–19	Psalms 114, **116**, 117 Ezekiel 3.12–end 2 Corinthians 3
Friday	**17 July** G	Isaiah 38.1–6, 21–22, 7–8 [sic] *Canticle:* Isaiah 38.10–16 or Psalm 32.1–8 Matthew 12.1–8	Psalm **139** 1 Samuel 3.1—4.1a Luke 20.20–26	Psalms **130**, 131, 137 Ezekiel 8 2 Corinthians 4
Saturday	**18 July** *Elizabeth Ferard, deaconess, founder of the* *Community of St Andrew, 1883* G	Micah 2.1–5 Psalm 10.1–5a, 12 Matthew 12.14–21	Psalms 120, **121**, 122 1 Samuel 4.1b–end Luke 20.27–40	Psalm **118** Ezekiel 9 2 Corinthians 5

Trinity 6

		Principal Service	3rd Service	2nd Service
Sunday 19 July **6th Sunday after Trinity** Proper 11	G	*Continuous:* Genesis 28.10–19a Psalm 139.1–11, 23–24 [or 139.1–11] Romans 8.12–25 Matthew 13.24–30, 36–43 / *Related:* Wisdom of Solomon 12.13, 16–19 or Isaiah 44.6–8 Psalm 86.11–end Romans 8.12–25 Matthew 13.24–30, 36–43	Psalm 71 Deuteronomy 30.1–10 1 Peter 3.8–18	Psalm 67 [70] 1 Kings 2.10–12; 3.16–28 Acts 4.1–22 *HC* Mark 6.30–34, 53–end
		Holy Communion	**Morning Prayer**	**Evening Prayer**
Monday 20 July *Margaret of Antioch, martyr, 4th cent. Bartolomé de las Casas, Apostle to the Indies, 1566* DEL week 16	G	Micah 6.1–4, 6–8 Psalm 50.3–7, 14 Matthew 12.38–42	Psalms 123, 124, 125, **126** 1 Samuel 5 Luke 20.41—21.4	Psalms **127**, 128, 129 Ezekiel 10.1–19 2 Corinthians 6.1—7.1
Tuesday 21 July	G	Micah 7.14–15, 18–20 Psalm 85.1–7 Matthew 12.46–end	Psalms **132**, 133 1 Samuel 6.1–16 Luke 21.5–19 *or:* 1st EP of Mary Magdalene: Psalm 139; Isaiah 25.1–9; 2 Corinthians 1.3–7	Psalms (134,) **135** Ezekiel 11.14–end 2 Corinthians 7.2–end
		Principal Service	**3rd Service**	**2nd Service**
Wednesday 22 July *Mary Magdalene*	W	Song of Solomon 3.1–4 Psalm 42.1–10 2 Corinthians 5.14–17 John 20.1–2, 11–18	*MP* Psalms 30, 32, 150 1 Samuel 16.14–end Luke 8.1–3	*EP* Psalm 63 Zephaniah 3.14–end Mark 15.40—16.7
		Holy Communion	**Morning Prayer**	**Evening Prayer**
Thursday 23 July *Bridget, abbess, 1373*	G	Jeremiah 2.1–3, 7–8, 12–13 Psalm 36.5–10 Matthew 13.10–17	Psalms 143, 146 1 Samuel 8 Luke 21.29–end	Psalms **138**, 140, 141 Ezekiel 12.17–end 2 Corinthians 8.16—9.5
Friday 24 July	G	Jeremiah 3.14–17 Psalm 23 or *Canticle:* Jeremiah 31.10–13 Matthew 13.18–23	Psalms 142, **144** 1 Samuel 9.1–14 Luke 22.1–13 *or:* 1st EP of James the Apostle: Psalm 144; Deuteronomy 30.11–end; Mark 5.21–end	Psalm **145** Ezekiel 13.1–16 2 Corinthians 9.6–end
		Principal Service	**3rd Service**	**2nd Service**
Saturday 25 July *James the Apostle*	R	Jeremiah 45.1–5 or Acts 11.27—12.2 Psalm 126 Acts 11.27—12.2 or 2 Corinthians 4.7–15 Matthew 20.20–28	*MP* Psalms 7, 29, 117 2 Kings 1.9–15 Luke 9.46–56	*EP* Psalm 94 Jeremiah 26.1–15 Mark 1.14–20

		Principal Service	3rd Service	2nd Service
Sunday	G **26 July** **7th Sunday after Trinity** Proper 12	*Continuous:* Genesis 29.15–28 Psalm 105.1–11, 45b [or 105.1–11] or Psalm 128 Romans 8.26–end Matthew 13.31–33, 44–52 *Related:* 1 Kings 3.5–12 Psalm 119.129–136	Psalm 77 Song of Solomon 2 or 1 Maccabees 2.[1–14] 15–22 1 Peter 4.7–14	Psalms 75 [76] 1 Kings 6.11–14, 23–end Acts 12.1–17 HC John 6.1–21
		Holy Communion	**Morning Prayer**	**Evening Prayer**
Monday	G **27 July** *Brooke Foss Westcott, bishop,* *teacher of the faith, 1901* DEL week 17	Jeremiah 13.1–11 Psalm 82 or Deuteronomy 32.18–21 Matthew 13.31–35	Psalms 1, 2, 3 1 Samuel 10.1–16 Luke 22.24–30	Psalms **4**, 7 Ezekiel 14.12–end 2 Corinthians 11.1–15
Tuesday	G **28 July**	Jeremiah 14.17–end Psalm 79.8–end Matthew 13.36–43	Psalms **5**, 6 (8) 1 Samuel 10.17–end Luke 22.31–38	Psalms **9**, 10* Ezekiel 18.1–20 2 Corinthians 11.16–end
Wednesday	Gw **29 July** *Mary, Martha and Lazarus,* *companions of Our Lord*	Jeremiah 15.10, 16–end Psalm 59.1–4, 18–end Matthew 13.44–46 *Lesser Festival eucharistic lectionary:* Isaiah 25.6–9 Psalm 49.5–10, 16 Hebrews 2.10–15 John 12.1–8	Psalm 119.**1–32** 1 Samuel 11 Luke 22.39–46	Psalms **11**, 12, 13 Ezekiel 18.21–32 2 Corinthians 12
Thursday	Gw **30 July** William Wilberforce, social reformer, Olaudah Equiano and Thomas Clarkson, anti-slavery campaigners, 1833, 1797 and 1846 (see p.83)	Jeremiah 18.1–6 Psalm 146.1–5 Matthew 13.47–53	Psalms **14**, **15**, 16 1 Samuel 12 Luke 22.47–62	Psalm **18** Ezekiel 20.1–20 2 Corinthians 13
Friday	G **31 July** *Ignatius of Loyola, founder of the* *Society of Jesus, 1556*	Jeremiah 26.1–9 Psalm 69.4–10 Matthew 13.54–end	Psalms 17, **19** 1 Samuel 13.5–18 Luke 22.63–end	Psalm **22** Ezekiel 20.21–38 James 1.1–11
Saturday	G **1 August**	Jeremiah 26.11–16, 24 Psalm 69.14–20 Matthew 14.1–12	Psalms 20, 21, **23** 1 Samuel 13.19—14.15 Luke 23.1–12	Psalms **24**, 25 Ezekiel 24.15–end James 1.12–end

		Principal Service	3rd Service	2nd Service
Sunday	**2 August** **8th Sunday after Trinity** Proper 13 — G	*Continuous:* Genesis 32.22–31 Psalm 17.1–7, 16 [or 17.1–7] *Related:* Isaiah 55.1–5 Psalm 145.8–9, 15–end [or 145.15–end] Romans 9.1–5 Matthew 14.13–21	Psalm 85 Song of Solomon 5.2–end or 1 Maccabees 3.1–12 2 Peter 1.1–15	Psalm 80 [or 80.1–8] 1 Kings 10.1–13 Acts 13.1–13 *HC* John 6.24–35
		Holy Communion	**Morning Prayer**	**Evening Prayer**
Monday	**3 August** DEL week 18 — G	Jeremiah 28 Psalm 119.89–96 Matthew 14.13–21	Psalms 27, **30** 1 Samuel 14.24–46 Luke 23.13–25	Psalms 26, **28**, 29 Ezekiel 28.1–19 James 2.1–13
Tuesday	**4 August** *Jean-Baptiste Vianney, curé d'Ars, spiritual guide, 1859* — G	Jeremiah 30.1–2, 12–15, 18–22 Psalm 102.16–21 Matthew 14.22–end or 15.1–2, 10–14	Psalms 32, **36** 1 Samuel 15.1–23 Luke 23.26–43	Psalm 33 Ezekiel 33.1–20 James 2.14–end
Wednesday	**5 August** Oswald, king, martyr, 642 (see p.79) — Gr	Jeremiah 31.1–7 Psalm 121 Matthew 15.21–28	Psalm 34 1 Samuel 16 Luke 23.44–56a	Psalm **119.33–56** Ezekiel 33.21–end James 3 *or:* 1st EP of the Transfiguration of Our Lord: Psalms 99, 110; Exodus 24.12–end; John 12.27–36a
		Principal Service	**3rd Service**	**2nd Service**
Thursday	**6 August** Transfiguration of Our Lord — *Gold or W*	Daniel 7.9–10, 13–14 Psalm 97 2 Peter 1.16–19 Luke 9.28–36	*MP* Psalms 27, 150 Ecclesiasticus 48.1–10 or 1 Kings 19.1–16 1 John 3.1–3	*EP* Psalm 72 Exodus 34.29–end 2 Corinthians 3
		Holy Communion	**Morning Prayer**	**Evening Prayer**
Friday	**7 August** *John Mason Neale, priest, hymn writer, 1866* — G	Nahum 2.1, 3.1–3, 6–7 Psalm 137.1–6 or Deuteronomy 32.35–36, 39, 41 Matthew 16.24–28	Psalm 31 1 Samuel 17.31–54 Luke 24.13–35	Psalm 35 Ezekiel 34.17–end James 4.13—5.6
Saturday	**8 August** Dominic, priest, founder of the Order of Preachers, 1221 (see p.82) — Gw	Habakkuk 1.12–2.4 Psalm 9.7–11 Matthew 17.14–20	Psalms 41, **42**, 43 1 Samuel 17.55—18.16 Luke 24.36–end	Psalms 45, **46** Ezekiel 36.16–36 James 5.7–end

Trinity 9

		Principal Service	3rd Service	2nd Service
Sunday	**9 August** **9th Sunday after Trinity** Proper 14 — G	*Continuous:* Genesis 37.1–4, 12–28; Psalm 105.1–6, 16–22, 45b [or 105.1–10] *Related:* 1 Kings 19.9–18; Psalm 85.8–13 Romans 10.5–15 Matthew 14.22–33	Psalm 88 Song of Solomon 8.5–7 or 1 Maccabees 14.4–15 2 Peter 3.8–13	Psalm 86 1 Kings 11.41—12.20 Acts 14.8–20 *HC* John 6.35, 41–51
		Holy Communion	**Morning Prayer**	**Evening Prayer**
Monday	**10 August** Laurence, deacon, martyr, 258 (see p.79) DEL week 19 — Gr	Ezekiel 1.2–5, 24–end Psalm 148.1–4, 12–13 Matthew 17.22–end	Psalm 44 1 Samuel 19.1–18 Acts 1.1–14	Psalms 47, 49 Ezekiel 37.1–14 Mark 1.1–13
Tuesday	**11 August** Clare of Assisi, founder of the Poor Clares, 1253 (see p.82) *John Henry Newman, priest, 1890* — Gw	Ezekiel 2.8—3.4 Psalm 119.65–72 Matthew 18.1–5, 10, 12–14	Psalms 48, 52 1 Samuel 20.1–17 Acts 1.15–end	Psalm 50 Ezekiel 37.15–end Mark 1.14–20
Wednesday	**12 August** — G	Ezekiel 9.1–7; 10.18–22 Psalm 113 Matthew 18.15–20	Psalm 119.57–80 1 Samuel 20.18–end Acts 2.1–21	Psalms 59, 60 (67) Ezekiel 39.21–end Mark 1.21–28
Thursday	**13 August** Jeremy Taylor, bishop, teacher of the faith, 1667 (see p.80) *Florence Nightingale, nurse, social reformer, 1910* *Octavia Hill, social reformer, 1912* — Gw	Ezekiel 12.1–12 Psalm 78.58–64 Matthew 18.21—19.1	Psalms 56, 57 (63*) 1 Samuel 21.1—22.5 Acts 2.22–36	Psalms 61, 62, 64 Ezekiel 43.1–12 Mark 1.29–end
Friday	**14 August** *Maximilian Kolbe, friar, martyr, 1941* — G	Ezekiel 16.1–15, 60–end Psalm 118.14–18 or *Canticle:* Song of Deliverance Matthew 19.3–12	Psalms 51, 54 1 Samuel 22.6–end Acts 2.37–end	Psalm 38 Ezekiel 44.4–16 Mark 2.1–12 *or:* 1st EP of the Blessed Virgin Mary: Psalm 72; Proverbs 8.22–31; John 19.23–27
		Principal Service	**3rd Service**	**2nd Service**
Saturday	**15 August** The Blessed Virgin Mary — W	Isaiah 61.10–end or Revelation 11.19—12.6, 10 Psalm 45.10–end Galatians 4.4–7 Luke 1.46–55	MP Psalm 98, 138, 147.1–12 Isaiah 7.10–15 Luke 11.27–28	EP Psalm 132 Song of Solomon 2.1–7 Acts 1.6–14

Trinity 10

		Principal Service		3rd Service	2nd Service
Sunday 16 August 10th Sunday after Trinity Proper 15	G	*Continuous:* Genesis 45.1–15 Psalm 133	*Related:* Isaiah 56.1,6–8 Psalm 67 Romans 11.1–2a,29–32 Matthew 15.[10–20] 21–28	Psalm 92 Jonah 1 or Ecclesiasticus 3.1–15 2 Peter 3.14–end	Psalm 90 [or 90.1–12] 2 Kings 4.1–37 Acts 16.1–15 *HC* John 6.51–58
		Holy Communion		**Morning Prayer**	**Evening Prayer**
Monday 17 August DEL week 20	G	Ezekiel 24.15–24 Psalm 78.1–8 Matthew 19.16–22		Psalm **71** 1 Samuel 24 Acts 3.11–end	Psalms **72**,75 Proverbs 1.1–19 Mark 2.23—3.6
Tuesday 18 August	G	Ezekiel 28.1–10 Psalm 107.1–3,40,43 Matthew 19.23–end		Psalm **73** 1 Samuel 26 Acts 4.1–12	Psalm **74** Proverbs 1.20–end Mark 3.7–19a
Wednesday 19 August	G	Ezekiel 34.1–11 Psalm 23 Matthew 20.1–16		Psalm **77** 1 Samuel 28.3–end Acts 4.13–31	Psalm 119.**81–104** Proverbs 2 Mark 3.19b–end
Thursday 20 August Bernard, abbot, teacher of the faith, 1153 (see p.80) *William and Catherine Booth, founders of the Salvation Army, 1912, 1890*	Gw	Ezekiel 36.23–28 Psalm 51.7–12 Matthew 22.1–14		Psalm **78.1–39*** 1 Samuel 31 Acts 4.32—5.11	Psalm **78.40–end*** Proverbs 3.1–26 Mark 4.1–20
Friday 21 August	G	Ezekiel 37.1–14 Psalm 107.1–8 Matthew 22.34–40		Psalm **55** 2 Samuel 1 Acts 5.12–26	Psalm **69** Proverbs 3.27—4.19 Mark 4.21–34
Saturday 22 August	G	Ezekiel 43.1–7 Psalm 85.7–end Matthew 23.1–12		Psalms **76**,79 2 Samuel 2.1–11 Acts 5.27–end	Psalms 81,**84** Proverbs 6.1–19 Mark 4.35–end

		Principal Service	3rd Service	2nd Service
Sunday	**23 August** G **11th Sunday after Trinity** Proper 16	*Continuous:* Exodus 1.8—2.10 Psalm 124 *Related:* Isaiah 51.1–6 Psalm 138 Romans 12.1–8 Matthew 16.13–20	Psalm 104.1–25 Jonah 2 or Ecclesiasticus 3.17–29 Revelation 1	Psalm 95 2 Kings 6.8–23 Acts 17.15–end HC John 6.56–69 *or:* 1st EP of Bartholomew the Apostle: Psalm 97; Isaiah 61.1–9; 2 Corinthians 6.1–10
Monday	**24 August** R Bartholomew the Apostle	Isaiah 43.8–13 or Acts 5.12–16 Psalm 145.1–7 Acts 5.12–16 or 1 Corinthians 4.9–15 Luke 22.24–30	MP Psalms 86, 117 Genesis 28.10–17 John 1.43–end	EP Psalms 91, 116 Ecclesiasticus 39.1–10 or Deuteronomy 18.15–19 Matthew 10.1–22
		Holy Communion	**Morning Prayer**	**Evening Prayer**
Tuesday	**25 August** G DEL week 21	2 Thessalonians 2.1–3a, 14–end Psalm 98 Matthew 23.23–26	Psalm 87, **89.1–18** 2 Samuel 5.1–12 Acts 7.1–16	Psalm **89.19–end** Proverbs 8.22–end Mark 5.21–34
Wednesday	**26 August** G	2 Thessalonians 3.6–10, 16–end Psalm 128 Matthew 23.27–32	Psalm 119.**105–128** 2 Samuel 6.1–19 Acts 7.17–43	Psalms **91**, 93 Proverbs 9 Mark 5.35–end
Thursday	**27 August** Gw Monica, mother of Augustine of Hippo, 387 (see p.83)	1 Corinthians 1.1–9 Psalm 145.1–7 Matthew 24.42–end	Psalms 90, **92** 2 Samuel 7.1–17 Acts 7.44–53	Psalm **94** Proverbs 10.1–12 Mark 6.1–13
Friday	**28 August** Gw Augustine, bishop, teacher of the faith, 430 (see p.80)	1 Corinthians 1.17–25 Psalm 33.6–12 Matthew 25.1–13	Psalms **88** (95) 2 Samuel 7.18–end Acts 7.54—8.3	Psalm **102** Proverbs 11.1–12 Mark 6.14–29
Saturday	**29 August** Gr Beheading of John the Baptist	1 Corinthians 1.26–end Psalm 33.12–15, 20–end Matthew 25.14–30 *Lesser Festival eucharistic lectionary:* Jeremiah 1.4–10 Psalm 11 Hebrews 11.32—12.2 Matthew 14.1–12	Psalms 96, **97**, 100 2 Samuel 9 Acts 8.4–25	Psalm **104** Proverbs 12.10–end Mark 6.30–44

54

		Principal Service		3rd Service	2nd Service
Sunday	**30 August** **12th Sunday after Trinity** Proper 17	G	*Continuous:* Exodus 3.1–15 Psalm 105.1–6, 23–26, 45b [or Psalm 115] Romans 12.9–end Matthew 16.21–end	*Related:* Jeremiah 15.15–21 Psalm 26.1–8	Psalm 107.1–32 Jonah 3.1–9 or Ecclesiasticus 11.7–28 (or 19–28) Revelation 3.14–end	Psalm 105.1–15 2 Kings 6.24–25; 7.3–end Acts 18.1–16 HC Mark 7.1–8, 14–15, 21–23
			Holy Communion	**Morning Prayer**	**Evening Prayer**
Monday	**31 August** Aidan, bishop, missionary, 651 (see p.82) DEL week 22	Gw	1 Corinthians 2.1–5 Psalm 33.12–21 Luke 4.16–30		Psalms **98**, 99, 101 2 Samuel 11 Acts 8.26–end	Psalm **105*** (or 103) Proverbs 14.31—15.17 Mark 6.45–end
Tuesday	**1 September** *Giles, hermit, c.710*	G	1 Corinthians 2.10b–end Psalm 145.10–17 Luke 4.31–37		Psalm **106*** (or 103) 2 Samuel 12.1–25 Acts 9.1–19a	Psalm **107*** Proverbs 15.18–end Mark 7.1–13
Wednesday	**2 September** *Martyrs of Papua New Guinea, 1901, 1942*	G	1 Corinthians 3.1–9 Psalm 62 Luke 4.38–end		Psalms 110, **111**, 112 2 Samuel 15.1–12 Acts 9.19b–31	Psalm 119.**129–152** Proverbs 18.10–end Mark 7.14–23
Thursday	**3 September** Gregory the Great, bishop, teacher of the faith, 604 (see p.80)	Gw	1 Corinthians 3.18–end Psalm 24.1–6 Luke 5.1–11		Psalms 113, **115** 2 Samuel 15.13–end Acts 9.32–end	Psalms 114, **116**, 117 Proverbs 20.1–22 Mark 7.24–30
Friday	**4 September** *Birinus, bishop, 650*	G	1 Corinthians 4.1–5 Psalm 37.3–8 Luke 5.33–end		Psalm **139** 2 Samuel 16.1–14 Acts 10.1–16	Psalms **130**, 131, 137 Proverbs 22.1–16 Mark 7.31–end
Saturday	**5 September**	G	1 Corinthians 4.6–15 Psalm 145.18–end Luke 6.1–5		Psalms 120, **121**, 122 2 Samuel 17.1–23 Acts 10.17–33	Psalm 118 Proverbs 24.23–end Mark 8.1–10

		Principal Service		3rd Service	2nd Service
Sunday	**6 September** G **13th Sunday after Trinity** Proper 18	*Continuous:* Exodus 12.1–14 Psalm 149	*Related:* Ezekiel 33.7–11 Psalm 119.33–40 Romans 13.8–end Matthew 18.15–20	Psalm 119.17–32 Jonah 3.10—4.11 or Ecclesiasticus 27.30—28.9 Revelation 8.1–5	Psalms 108 [115] Ezekiel 12.21—13.16 Acts 19.1–20 *HC* Mark 7.24–end
		Holy Communion		**Morning Prayer**	**Evening Prayer**
Monday	**7 September** G DEL week 23	1 Corinthians 5.1–8 Psalm 5.5–9a Luke 6.6–11		Psalms 123, 124, 125, **126** 2 Samuel 18.1–18 Acts 10.34–end	Psalms **127**, 128, 129 Proverbs 25.1–14 Mark 8.11–21
Tuesday	**8 September** Gw Birth of the Blessed Virgin Mary (see p.79)	1 Corinthians 6.1–11 Psalm 149.1–5 Luke 6.12–19		Psalms **132**, 133 2 Samuel 18.19—19.8a Acts 11.1–18	Psalms (134,) **135** Proverbs 25.15–end Mark 8.22–26
Wednesday	**9 September** G *Charles Fuge Lowder, priest, 1880*	1 Corinthians 7.25–31 Psalm 45.11–end Luke 6.20–26		Psalm 119.**153–end** 2 Samuel 19.8b–23 Acts 11.19–end	Psalm **136** Proverbs 26.12–end Mark 8.27—9.1
Thursday	**10 September** G	1 Corinthians 8.1–7, 11–end Psalm 139.1–9 Luke 6.27–38		Psalms **143**, 146 2 Samuel 19.24–end Acts 12.1–17	Psalms **138**, 140, 141 Proverbs 27.1–22 Mark 9.2–13
Friday	**11 September** G	1 Corinthians 9.16–19, 22–end Psalm 84.1–6 Luke 6.39–42		Psalms 142, **144** 2 Samuel 23.1–7 Acts 12.18–end	Psalm **145** Proverbs 30.1–9, 24–31 Mark 9.14–29
Saturday	**12 September** G	1 Corinthians 10.14–22 Psalm 116.10–end Luke 6.43–end		Psalm **147** 2 Samuel 24 Acts 13.1–12	Psalms **148**, 149, 150 Proverbs 31.10–end Mark 9.30–37

Trinity 14

		Principal Service	3rd Service	2nd Service
Sunday	13 September G **14th Sunday after Trinity** Proper 19	*Continuous:* Exodus 14.19–end Psalm 114 or *Canticle:* Exodus 15.1b–11, 20–21 Romans 14.1–12 Matthew 18.21–35 *Related:* Genesis 50.15–21 Psalm 103.1–13 [or 103.8–13]	Psalm 119.65–88 Isaiah 44.24—45.8 Revelation 12.1–12	Psalm 119.41–48 [49–64] Ezekiel 20.1–8, 33–44 Acts 20.17–end HC Mark 8.27–end or: 1st EP of Holy Cross Day: Psalm 66; Isaiah 52.13—end of 53; Ephesians 2.11–end
Monday	14 September R Holy Cross Day	Numbers 21.4–9 Psalm 22.23–28 Philippians 2.6–11 John 3.13–17	MP Psalms 2, 8, 146 Genesis 3.1–15 John 12.27–36a	EP Psalms 110, 150 Isaiah 63.1–16 1 Corinthians 1.18–25

		Holy Communion	Morning Prayer	Evening Prayer
Tuesday	15 September Gr Cyprian, bishop, martyr, 258 (see p.79) DEL week 24	1 Corinthians 12.12–14, 27–end Psalm 100 Luke 7.11–17	Psalms 5, 6 (8) 1 Kings 1.32—2.4; 2.10–12 Acts 13.44—14.7	Psalms 9, 10* Wisdom 2 or 1 Chronicles 13 Mark 10.1–16
Wednesday	16 September Gw Ninian, bishop, apostle of the Picts, c.432 (see p.82) *Edward Bouverie Pusey, priest, 1882*	1 Corinthians 12.31b—end of 13 Psalm 33.1–12 Luke 7.31–35	Psalm 119.1–32 1 Kings 3 Acts 14.8–end	Psalms 11, 12, 13 Wisdom 3.1–9 or 1 Chronicles 15.1—16.3 Mark 10.17–31
Thursday	17 September Gw Hildegard, abbess, visionary, 1179 (see p.82)	1 Corinthians 15.1–11 Psalm 118.1–2, 17–20 Luke 7.36–end	Psalms 14, 15, 16 1 Kings 4.29—5.12 Acts 15.1–21	Psalm 18* Wisdom 4.7–end or 1 Chronicles 17 Mark 10.32–34
Friday	18 September G	1 Corinthians 15.12–20 Psalm 17.1–8 Luke 8.1–3	Psalms 17, 19 1 Kings 6.1, 11–28 Acts 15.22–35	Psalm 22 Wisdom 5.1–16 or 1 Chronicles 21.1—22.1 Mark 10.35–45
Saturday	19 September G *Theodore, archbishop, 690*	1 Corinthians 15.35–37, 42–49 Psalm 30.1–5 Luke 8.4–15	Psalms 20, 21, 23 1 Kings 8.1–30 Acts 15.36—16.5	Psalms 24, 25 Wisdom 5.17—6.11 or 1 Chronicles 22.2–end Mark 10.46–end

Trinity 15

	Principal Service	3rd Service	2nd Service
Sunday **20 September** 15th Sunday after Trinity Proper 20 *G*	*Continuous:* Exodus 16.2–15 Psalm 105.1–6, 37–end [or 105.37–end] *Related:* Jonah 3.10–end of 4 Psalm 145.1–8 Philippians 1.21–end Matthew 20.1–16	Psalm 119.153–end Isaiah 45.9–22 Revelation 14.1–5	Psalm 119.113–136 [or 119.121–[128] Ezekiel 33.23, 30—34.10 Acts 26.1, 9–25 HC Mark 9.30–37 *or:* 1st EP of Matthew, Apostle and Evangelist: Psalm 34: Isaiah 33.13–17; Matthew 6.19–end
Monday **21 September** Matthew, Apostle and Evangelist *R*	Proverbs 3.13–18 Psalm 119.65–72 2 Corinthians 4.1–6 Matthew 9.9–13	MP Psalms 49, 117 1 Kings 19.15–end 2 Timothy 3.14–end	EP Psalm 119.33–40, 89–96 Ecclesiastes 5.4–12 Matthew 19.16–end
Tuesday **22 September** DEL week 25 *G*	**Holy Communion** Proverbs 21.1–6, 10–13 Psalm 119.1–8 Luke 8.19–21	**Morning Prayer** Psalms 32, 36 1 Kings 8.63—9.9 Acts 16.25–end	**Evening Prayer** Psalm 33 Wisdom 7.1–14 or 1 Chronicles 28.11–end Mark 11.12–26
Wednesday **23 September** Ember Day *G*	Proverbs 30.5–9 Psalm 119.105–112 Luke 9.1–6	Psalm 34 1 Kings 10.1–25 Acts 17.1–15	Psalm 119.33–56 Wisdom 7.15—8.4 or 1 Chronicles 29.1–9 Mark 11.27–end
Thursday **24 September** *G*	Ecclesiastes 1.2–11 Psalm 90.1–6 Luke 9.7–9	Psalm 37* 1 Kings 11.1–13 Acts 17.16–end	Psalms 39, 40 Wisdom 8.5–18 or 1 Chronicles 29.10–20 Mark 12.1–12
Friday **25 September** Lancelot Andrewes, bishop, spiritual writer, 1626 (see p.81) Sergei of Radonezh, monastic reformer, teacher of the faith, 1392 Ember Day *Gw*	Ecclesiastes 3.1–11 Psalm 144.1–4 Luke 9.18–22	Psalm 31 1 Kings 11.26–end Acts 18.1–21	Psalm 35 Wisdom 8.21—end of 9 or 1 Chronicles 29.21–end Mark 12.13–17
Saturday **26 September** Wilson Carlile, founder of the Church Army, 1942 Ember Day *G*	Ecclesiastes 11.9—12.8 Psalm 90.1–2, 12–end Luke 9.43b–45	Psalms 41, **42**, 43 1 Kings 12.1–24 Acts 18.22—19.7	Psalms 45, **46** Wisdom 10.15—11.10 or 2 Chronicles 1.1–13 Mark 12.18–27

Day		Principal Service	3rd Service	2nd Service
Sunday	27 September G **16th Sunday after Trinity** Proper 21	*Continuous:* Exodus 17.1–7 Psalm 78.1–4, 12–16 [or 78.1–7] *Related:* Ezekiel 18.1–4, 25–end Psalm 25.1–8 Philippians 2.1–13 Matthew 21.23–32	Psalms 125, 126, **127** Isaiah 48.12–21 Luke 11.37–54	Psalms [120, 123] 124 Ezekiel 37.15–end 1 John 2.22–end HC Mark 9.38–end

Day		Holy Communion	Morning Prayer	Evening Prayer
Monday	28 September G DEL week 26	Job 1.6–end Psalm 17.1–11 Luke 9.46–50	Psalm **44** 1 Kings 12.25—13.10 Acts 19.8–20	Psalms **47**, 49 Wisdom 11.21—12.2 or 2 Chronicles 2.1–16 Mark 12.28–34 or: 1st EP of Michael and All Angels: Psalm 91; 2 Kings 6.8–17; Matthew 18.1–6, 10

Day		Principal Service	3rd Service	2nd Service
Tuesday	29 September W Michael and All Angels	Genesis 28.10–17 or Revelation 12.7–12 Psalm 103.19–end Revelation 12.7–12 or Hebrews 1.5–end John 1.47–end	MP Psalms 34, 150 Tobit 12.6–end or Daniel 12.1–4 Acts 12.1–11	EP Psalms 138, 148 Daniel 10.4–end Revelation 5

Day		Holy Communion	Morning Prayer	Evening Prayer
Wednesday	30 September G *Jerome, translator, teacher of the faith, 420*	Job 9.1–12, 14–16 Psalm 88.1–6, 11 Luke 9.57–end	Psalm **119.57–80** 1 Kings 17 Acts 20.1–16	Psalms **59**, 60 (67) Wisdom 13.1–9 or 2 Chronicles 5 Mark 13.1–13
Thursday	1 October G *Remigius, bishop, 533* *Anthony Ashley Cooper (Earl of Shaftesbury),* *social reformer, 1885*	Job 19.21–27a Psalm 27.13–16 Luke 10.1–12	Psalms 56, **57** (63*) 1 Kings 18.1–20 Acts 20.17–end	Psalms 61, **62**, 64 Wisdom 16.15—17.1 or 2 Chronicles 6.1–21 Mark 13.14–23
Friday	2 October G	Job 38.1, 12–21; 40.3–5 Psalm 139.6–11 Luke 10.13–16	Psalms **51**, 54 1 Kings 18.21–end Acts 21.1–16	Psalm **38** Wisdom 18.6–19 or 2 Chronicles 6.22–end Mark 13.24–31
Saturday	3 October G *George Bell, bishop, ecumenist, peacemaker,* *1958*	Job 42.1–3, 6, 12–end Psalm 119.169–end Luke 10.17–24	Psalm **68** 1 Kings 19 Acts 21.17–36	Psalms 65, **66** Wisdom 19 or 2 Chronicles 7 Mark 13.32–end

	Principal Service	3rd Service	2nd Service
Sunday **4 October** 17th Sunday after Trinity Proper 22 G	Continuous: Exodus 20.1–4, 7–9, 12–20 Psalm 19 [or 19.7–end] Philippians 3.4b–14 Matthew 21.33–end *Related:* Isaiah 5.1–7 Psalm 80.9–17	Psalms 128, 129, 134 Isaiah 49.13–23 Luke 12.1–12	Psalm 136 [or 136.1–9] Proverbs 2.1–11 1 John 2.1–17 HC Mark 10.2–16
	Holy Communion	**Morning Prayer**	**Evening Prayer**
Monday **5 October** DEL week 27 G	Galatians 1.6–12 Psalm 111.1–6 Luke 10.25–37	Psalm 71 1 Kings 21 Acts 21.37—22.21	Psalms 72, 75 1 Maccabees 1.1–19 or 2 Chronicles 9.1–12 Mark 14.1–11
Tuesday **6 October** William Tyndale, translator, martyr, 1536 (see p.79) Gr	Galatians 1.13–end Psalm 139.1–9 Luke 10.38–end	Psalm 73 1 Kings 22.1–28 Acts 22.22—23.11	Psalm 74 1 Maccabees 1.20–40 or 2 Chronicles 10.1—11.4 Mark 14.12–25
Wednesday **7 October** G	Galatians 2.1–2, 7–14 Psalm 117 Luke 11.1–4	Psalm 77 1 Kings 22.29–45 Acts 23.12–end	Psalm 119.81–104 1 Maccabees 1.41–end or 2 Chronicles 12 Mark 14.26–42
Thursday **8 October** G	Galatians 3.1–5 Canticle: Benedictus Luke 11.5–13	Psalm 78.1–39* 2 Kings 1.2–17 Acts 24.1–23	Psalm 78.40–end* 1 Maccabees 2.1–28 or 2 Chronicles 13.1—14.1 Mark 14.43–52
Friday **9 October** Denys, bishop, and companions, martyrs, c.250; Robert Grosseteste, bishop, philosopher, scientist, 1253 G	Galatians 3.7–14 Psalm 111.4–end Luke 11.15–26	Psalm 55 2 Kings 2.1–18 Acts 24.24—25.12	Psalm 69 1 Maccabees 2.29–48 or 2 Chronicles 14.2–end Mark 14.53–65
Saturday **10 October** Paulinus, bishop, missionary, 644 (see p.82) Thomas Traherne, poet, spiritual writer, 1674 Gw	Galatians 3.22–end Psalm 105.1–7 Luke 11.27–28	Psalms 76, 79 2 Kings 4.1–37 Acts 25.13–end	Psalms 81, 84 1 Maccabees 2.49–end or 2 Chronicles 15.1–15 Mark 14.66–end

Trinity 18

		Principal Service		3rd Service	2nd Service
Sunday	**11 October** **18th Sunday after Trinity** Proper 23 G	*Continuous:* Exodus 32.1–14 Psalm 106.1–6, 19–23 [or 106.1–6]	*Related:* Isaiah 25.1–9 Psalm 23 Philippians 4.1–9 Matthew 22.1–14	Psalms 138, 141 Isaiah 50.4–10 Luke 13.22–30	Psalm 139.1–18 [or 139.1–11] Proverbs 3.1–18 1 John 3.1–15 HC Mark 10.17–31
		Holy Communion		**Morning Prayer**	**Evening Prayer**
Monday	**12 October** Gw Wilfrid, bishop, missionary, 709 (see p.82) *Elizabeth Fry, prison reformer, 1845* *Edith Cavell, nurse, 1915* DEL week 28	Galatians 4.21–24, 26–27, 31; 5.1 Ps 113 Luke 11.29–32		Psalms 80, 82 2 Kings 5 Acts 26.1–23	Psalms 85, 86 1 Maccabees 3.1–26 or 2 Chronicles 17.1–12 Mark 15.1–15
Tuesday	**13 October** Gw Edward the Confessor, king, 1066 (see p.83)	Galatians 5.1–6 Psalm 119.41–48 Luke 11.37–41		Psalms 87, **89.1–18** 2 Kings 6.1–23 Acts 26.24–end	Psalm **89.19–end** 1 Maccabees 3.27–41 or 2 Chronicles 18.1–27 Mark 15.16–32
Wednesday	**14 October** G	Galatians 5.18–end Psalm 1 Luke 11.42–46		Psalms **119.105–128** 2 Kings 9.1–16 Acts 27.1–26	Psalms **91**, 93 1 Maccabees 3.42–end or 2 Chronicles 18.28—end of 19 Mark 15.33–41
Thursday	**15 October** Gw Teresa of Avila, teacher of the faith, 1582 (see p.80)	Ephesians 1.1–10 Psalm 98.1–4 Luke 11.47–end		Psalms 90, **92** 2 Kings 9.17–end Acts 27.27–end	Psalm **94** 1 Maccabees 4.1–25 or 2 Chronicles 20.1–23 Mark 15.42–end
Friday	**16 October** G *Nicholas Ridley and Hugh Latimer,* *bishops, martyrs, 1555*	Ephesians 1.11–14 Psalm 33.1–6, 12 Luke 12.1–7		Psalms **88** (95) 2 Kings 12.1–19 Acts 28.1–16	Psalm **102** 1 Maccabees 4.26–35 or 2 Chronicles 22.10—end of 23 Mark 16.1–8
Saturday	**17 October** Gr Ignatius, bishop, martyr, c.107 (see p.79)	Ephesians 1.15–end Psalm 8 Luke 12.8–12		Psalms 96, **97**, 100 2 Kings 17.1–23 Acts 28.17–end	Psalm **104** 1 Maccabees 4.36–end or 2 Chronicles 24.1–22 Mark 16.9–end

or, if Luke the Evangelist is celebrated on Sunday 18 October:
1st EP of Luke the Evangelist:
Psalm 33; Hosea 6.1–3; 2 Timothy 3.10–end

If Luke the Evangelist is celebrated on Sunday 18 October:

		Principal Service	3rd Service	2nd Service
Sunday	**18 October** R	Isaiah 35.3–6 or Acts 16.6–12a	MP Psalms 145, 146	EP Psalm 103
	Luke the Evangelist	Psalm 147.1–7	Isaiah 55	Ecclesiasticus 38.1–14
		2 Timothy 4.5–17	Luke 1.1–4	or Isaiah 61.1–6
		Luke 10.1–9		Colossians 4.7–end

		Holy Communion	Morning Prayer	Evening Prayer
Monday	**19 October** Gw	Ephesians 2.1–10	Psalms **98**, 99, 101	Psalm **105*** (or 103)
	Henry Martyn, translator,	Psalm 100	2 Kings 17.24–end	1 Maccabees 6.1–17
	missionary, 1812 (see p.82)	Luke 12.13–21	Philippians 1.1–11	or 2 Chronicles 26.1–21
	DEL week 29			John 13.1–11

If Luke the Evangelist is transferred to Monday 19 October:

		Principal Service	3rd Service	2nd Service
Sunday	**18 October** G	*Continuous:*	*Related:*	Psalms 142 [143.1–11]	Psalms 145, 149	Psalms 142 [143.1–11]
	19th Sunday after Trinity	Exodus 33.12–end	Isaiah 45.1–7		Isaiah 54.1–14	Proverbs 4.1–18
	Proper 24	Psalm 99	Psalm 96.1–9 [10–end]		Luke 13.31–end	1 John 3.16—4.6
			1 Thessalonians 1.1–10			HC Mark 10.35–45
			Matthew 22.15–22			*or:* 1st EP of Luke the Evangelist:
						Psalm 33; Hosea 6.1–3;
						2 Timothy 3.10–end

		Principal Service	3rd Service	2nd Service
Monday	**19 October** R	Isaiah 35.3–6 or Acts 16.6–12a	MP Psalms 145, 146	EP Psalm 103
	Luke the Evangelist	Psalm 147.1–7	Isaiah 55	Ecclesiasticus 38.1–14
	(transferred from 18 October)	2 Timothy 4.5–17	Luke 1.1–4	or Isaiah 61.1–6
		Luke 10.1–9		Colossians 4.7–end

		Holy Communion	Morning Prayer	Evening Prayer
Tuesday 20 October DEL week 29	G	Ephesians 2.12–end Psalm 85.7–end Luke 12.35–38	Psalm **106*** (or 103) 2 Kings 18.1–12 Philippians 1.12–end	Psalm **107*** 1 Maccabees 6.18–47 or 2 Chronicles 28 John 13.12–20
Wednesday 21 October	G	Ephesians 3.2–12 Psalm 98 Luke 12.39–48	Psalms 110, **111**, 112 2 Kings 18.13–end Philippians 2.1–13	Psalm **119.129–152** 1 Maccabees 7.1–20 or 2 Chronicles 29.1–19 John 13.21–30
Thursday 22 October	G	Ephesians 3.14–end Psalm 33.1–6 Luke 12.49–53	Psalms 113, **115** 2 Kings 19.1–19 Philippians 2.14–end	Psalms 114, **116**, 117 1 Maccabees 7.21–end or 2 Chronicles 29.20–end John 13.31–end
Friday 23 October	G	Ephesians 4.1–6 Psalm 24.1–6 Luke 12.54–end	Psalm **139** 2 Kings 19.20–36 Philippians 3.1—4.1	Psalms **130**, 131, 137 1 Maccabees 9.1–22 or 2 Chronicles 30 John 14.1–14
Saturday 24 October	G	Ephesians 4.7–16 Psalm 122 Luke 13.1–9	Psalms 120, **121**, 122 2 Kings 20 Philippians 4.2–end	Psalm **118** 1 Maccabees 13.41–end; 14.4–15 or 2 Chronicles 32.1–22 John 14.15–end

		Principal Service		3rd Service	2nd Service
Sunday	**25 October** **Last Sunday after Trinity** Proper 25	G	*Continuous:* Deuteronomy 34.1–12 Psalm 90.1–6, 13–end [or 90.1–6]	*Related:* Leviticus 19.1–2, 15–18 Psalm 1	Psalm 119.137–152 Isaiah 59.9–20 Luke 14.1–14	Psalm 119.89–104 Ecclesiastes 11, 12 2 Timothy 2.1–7 HC Mark 12.28–34
			1 Thessalonians 2.1–8 Matthew 22.34–end			
or **Sunday**	**25 October** **Bible Sunday**	G	Nehemiah 8.1–4a [5–6] 8–12 Psalm 119. 9–16 Colossians 3.12–17 Matthew 24.30–35		Psalm 119. 137–152 Deuteronomy 17.14–15, 18–end John 5.36b–end	Psalm 119.89–104 Isaiah 55.1–11 Luke 4.14–30

or, if the date of dedication of a church is not known, the Dedication Festival (Gold or W) may be celebrated today or on 4 October, or on a suitable date chosen locally (see p.77).

			Holy Communion	Morning Prayer	Evening Prayer
Monday	**26 October** Alfred, king, scholar, 899 (see p.83) Cedd, abbot, bishop, 664 DEL week 30	Gw	Ephesians 4.32—5.8 Psalm 1 Luke 13.10–17	Psalms 123, 124, 125, **126** 2 Kings 21.1–18 1 Timothy 1.1–17	Psalms **127**, 128, 129 2 Maccabees 4.7–17 or 2 Chronicles 33.1–13 John 15.1–11
Tuesday	**27 October**	G	Ephesians 5.21–end Psalm 128 Luke 13.18–21	Psalms **132, 133** 2 Kings 22.1—23.3 1 Timothy 1.18—end of 2	Psalms (134), **135** 2 Maccabees 6.12–end or 2 Chronicles 34.1–18 John 15.12–17
					or: 1st EP of Simon and Jude, Apostles: Psalms 124, 125, 126; Deuteronomy 32.1–4; John 14.15–26

		Principal Service	3rd Service	2nd Service
Wednesday	**28 October** R Simon and Jude, Apostles	Isaiah 28.14–16 Psalm 119.89–96 Ephesians 2.19–end John 15.17–end	*MP* Psalms 116, 117 Wisdom 5.1–16 or Isaiah 45.18–end Luke 6.12–16	*EP* Psalm 119.1–16 1 Maccabees 2.42–66 or Jeremiah 3.11–18 Jude 1–4, 17–end
		Holy Communion	**Morning Prayer**	**Evening Prayer**
Thursday	**29 October** Gr James Hannington, bishop, martyr, 1885 (see p.79)	Ephesians 6.10–20 Psalm 144.1–2, 9–11 Luke 13.31–end	Psalms 143, 146 2 Kings 23.36—24.17 1 Timothy 4	Psalms 138, 140, 141 2 Maccabees 7.20–41 or 2 Chronicles 35.1–19 John 16.1–15
Friday	**30 October** G	Philippians 1.1–11 Psalm 111 Luke 14.1–6	Psalms 142, 144 2 Kings 24.18—25.12 1 Timothy 5.1–16	Psalm 145 Tobit 1 or 2 Chronicles 35.20—36.10 John 16.16–22
Saturday	**31 October** G *Martin Luther, reformer, 1546*	Philippians 1.18–26 Psalm 42.1–7 Luke 14.1, 7–11	Psalm 147 2 Kings 25.22–end 1 Timothy 5.17–end	**1st EP of All Saints' Day** Psalms 1, 5 Ecclesiasticus 44.1–15 or Isaiah 40.27–end Revelation 19.6–10

			Principal Service	3rd Service	2nd Service
Sunday	**1 November** **All Saints' Day**	*Gold or W*	Revelation 7.9–end Psalm 34.1–10 1 John 3.1–3 Matthew 5.1–12	MP Psalms 15, 84, 149 Isaiah 35 Luke 9.18–27	EP Psalms 148, 150 Isaiah 65.17–end Hebrews 11.32—12.2
			Holy Communion	Morning Prayer	Evening Prayer
Monday	**2 November** Commemoration of the Faithful Departed (All Souls' Day) DEL week 31	*Rp/Gp*	Philippians 2.1–4 Psalm 131 Luke 14.12–14 *Lesser Festival eucharistic lectionary:* Lamentations 3.17–26, 31–33 *or* Wisdom 3.1–9 Psalm 23 *or* 27.1–6, 16–end Romans 5.5–11 *or* 1 Peter 1.3–9 John 5.19–25 *or* John 6.37–40	Psalms 2, 146 *or* 1, 2, 3 Daniel 1 Revelation 1	Psalms 92, 96, 97 *or* 4, 7 Isaiah 1.1–20 Matthew 1.18–end
Tuesday	**3 November** Richard Hooker, priest, teacher of the faith, 1600 (see p.80) *Martin of Porres, friar, 1639*	*Rw/Gw*	Philippians 2.5–11 Psalm 22.22–27 Luke 14.15–24	Psalms 5, 147.1–12 *or* 5, 6 (8) Daniel 2.1–24 Revelation 2.1–11	Psalms 98, 99, **100** *or* **9**, 10 Isaiah 1.21–end Matthew 2.1–15
Wednesday	**4 November**	*R/G*	Philippians 2.12–18 Psalm 27.1–5 Luke 14.25–33	Psalms **9**, 147.13–end *or* **119.1–32** Daniel 2.25–end Revelation 2.12–end	Psalm 111, **112**, 116 *or* **11**, 12, 13 Isaiah 2.1–11 Matthew 2.16–end
Thursday	**5 November**	*R/G*	Philippians 3.3–8*a* Psalm 105.1–7 Luke 15.1–10	Psalms 11, **15**, 148 *or* 14, **15**, 16 Daniel 3.1–18 Revelation 3.1–13	Psalm **118** *or* **18*** Isaiah 2.12–end Matthew 3
Friday	**6 November** *Leonard, hermit, 6th cent.* *William Temple, archbishop,* *teacher of the faith, 1944*	*R/G*	Philippians 3.17—4.1 Psalm 122 Luke 16.1–8	Psalms **16**, 149 *or* 17, **19** Daniel 3.19–end Revelation 3.14–end	Psalms 137, 138, **143** *or* **22** Isaiah 3.1–15 Matthew 4.1–11
Saturday	**7 November** Willibrord, bishop, 739 (see p.82)	*Rw/Gw*	Philippians 4.10–19 Psalm 112 Luke 16.9–15	Psalms **18.31–end**, 150 *or* 20, 21, **23** Daniel 4.1–18 Revelation 4	Psalm **145** *or* **24**, 25 Isaiah 4.2—5.7 Matthew 4.12–22

		Principal Service	3rd Service	2nd Service
Sunday	**8 November** R/G **3rd Sunday before Advent** *Remembrance Sunday*	Wisdom of Solomon 6.12–16 Canticle: Wisdom of Solomon 6.17–20 or Amos 5.18–24 Psalm 70 1 Thessalonians 4.13–end Matthew 25.1–13	Psalm 91 Deuteronomy 17.14–end 1 Timothy 2.1–7	Psalms [20] 82 Judges 7.2–22 John 15.9–17
		Holy Communion	**Morning Prayer**	**Evening Prayer**
Monday	**9 November** R/G *Margery Kempe, mystic, c.1440* DEL week 32	Titus 1.1–9 Psalm 24.1–6 Luke 17.1–6	Psalms 19, **20** or 27, **30** Daniel 4.19–end Revelation 5	Psalm **34** or 26, **28**, 29 Isaiah 5.8–24 Matthew 4.23—5.12
Tuesday	**10 November** Rw/Gw Leo the Great, bishop, teacher of the faith, 461 (see p.80)	Titus 2.1–8, 11–14 Psalm 37.3–5, 30–32 Luke 17.7–10	Psalms **21**, 24 or 32, **36** Daniel 5.1–12 Revelation 6	Psalms 36, **40** or **33** Isaiah 5.25–end Matthew 5.13–20
Wednesday	**11 November** Rw/Gw Martin, bishop, c.397 (see p.81)	Titus 3.1–7 Psalm 23 Luke 17.11–19	Psalms **23**, 25 or **34** Daniel 5.13–end Revelation 7.1–4, 9–end	Psalm **37** or **119.33–56** Isaiah 6 Matthew 5.21–37
Thursday	**12 November** R/G	Philemon 7–20 Psalm 146.4–end Luke 17.20–25	Psalms **26**, 27 or **37*** Daniel 6 Revelation 8	Psalms 42, **43** or 39, **40** Isaiah 7.1–17 Matthew 5.38–end
Friday	**13 November** Rw/Gw Charles Simeon, priest, evangelical divine, 1836 (see p.81)	2 John 4–9 Psalm 119.1–8 Luke 17.26–end	Psalms 28, **32** or 31 Daniel 7.1–14 Revelation 9.1–12	Psalm **31** or **35** Isaiah 8.1–15 Matthew 6.1–18
Saturday	**14 November** R/G *Samuel Seabury, bishop, 1796*	3 John 5–8 Psalm 112 Luke 18.1–8	Psalms **33** or 41, **42**, 43 Daniel 7.15–end Revelation 9.13–end	Psalm 84, **86** or 45, **46** Isaiah 8.16—9.7 Matthew 6.19–end

2 before Advent

		Principal Service	3rd Service	2nd Service
Sunday	**15 November** R/G **2nd Sunday before Advent**	Zephaniah 1.7, 12-end Psalm 90.1-8 [9-11] 12 [or 90.1-8] 1 Thessalonians 5.1-11 Matthew 25.14-30	Psalm 98 Daniel 10.19-end Revelation 4	Psalm 89.19-37 [or 89.19-29] 1 Kings 1.15-40 (or 1-40) Revelation 1.4-18 HC Luke 9.1-6
		Holy Communion	*Morning Prayer*	*Evening Prayer*
Monday	**16 November** Rw/Gw Margaret, queen, philanthropist, 1093 (see p.83) *Edmund Rich, archbishop, 1240* DEL week 33	Revelation 1.1-4, 2.1-5 Psalm 1 Luke 18.35-end	Psalms 46, **47** or **44** Daniel 8.1-14 Revelation 10	Psalms 70, **71** or **47**, 49 Isaiah 9.8-10.4 Matthew 7.1-12
Tuesday	**17 November** Rw/Gw Hugh, bishop, 1200 (see p.81)	Revelation 3.1-6, 14-end Psalm 15 Luke 19.1-10	Psalms 48, **52** or **48**, 52 Daniel 8.15-end Revelation 11.1-14	Psalms **67**, 72 or **50** Isaiah 10.5-19 Matthew 7.13-end
Wednesday	**18 November** Rw/Gw Elizabeth, princess, philanthropist, 1231 (see p.83)	Revelation 4 Psalm 150 Luke 19.11-28	Psalms **56**, 57 or **119.57-80** Daniel 9.1-19 Revelation 11.15-end	Psalm **73** or **59**, 60 (67) Isaiah 10.20-32 Matthew 8.1-13
Thursday	**19 November** Rw/Gw Hilda, abbess, 680 (see p.82) *Mechtild, béguine, mystic, 1280*	Revelation 5.1-10 Psalm 149.1-5 Luke 19.41-44	Psalms 61, **62** or 56, **57** (63*) Daniel 9.20-end Revelation 12	Psalms 74, **76** or 61, **62**, 64 Isaiah 10.33—11.9 Matthew 8.14-22
Friday	**20 November** R/Gr Edmund, king, martyr, 870 (see p.79) *Priscilla Lydia Sellon, a restorer of the* *religious life in the Church of England, 1876*	Revelation 10.8-11 Psalm 119.65-72 Luke 19.45-48	Psalms **63**, 65 or **51**, 54 Daniel 10.1—11.1 Revelation 13.1-10	Psalm **77** or **38** Isaiah 11.10-end of 12 Matthew 8.23-end
Saturday	**21 November** R/G	Revelation 11.4-12 Psalm 144.1-9 Luke 20.27-40	Psalm **78.1-39** or **68** Daniel 12 Revelation 13.11-end	Psalm **78.40-end** or 65, **66** Isaiah 13.1-13 Matthew 9.1-17 *or:* 1st EP of Christ the King: Psalms 99, 100; Isaiah 10.33—11.9; 1 Timothy 6.11-16

			Principal Service	3rd Service	2nd Service
Sunday	**22 November** Christ the King *Sunday next before Advent*	R/W	Ezekiel 34.11–16, 20–24 Psalm 95.1–7 Ephesians 1.15–end Matthew 25.31–end	MP Psalms 29, 110 Isaiah 4.2—5.7 Luke 19.29–38	EP Psalms 93 [97] 2 Samuel 23.1–7 or 1 Maccabees 2.15–29 Matthew 28.16–end
			Holy Communion	**Morning Prayer**	**Evening Prayer**
Monday	**23 November** Clement, bishop, martyr, c.100 (see p.79) DEL week 34	R/Gr	Revelation 14.1–5 Psalm 24.1–6 Luke 21.1–4	Psalms 92, **96** or **71** Isaiah 40.1–11 Revelation 14.1–13	Psalms **80**, 81 or **72**, 75 Isaiah 14.3–20 Matthew 9.18–34
Tuesday	**24 November**	R/G	Revelation 14.14–19 Psalm 96 Luke 21.5–11	Psalms **97**, 98, 100 or **73** Isaiah 40.12–26 Revelation 14.14—end of 15	Psalms 99, **101** or **74** Isaiah 17 Matthew 9.35—10.15
Wednesday	**25 November** *Catherine, martyr, 4th cent.* *Isaac Watts, hymn writer, 1748*	R/G	Revelation 15.1–4 Psalm 98 Luke 21.12–19	Psalms 110, 111, **112** or **77** Isaiah 40.27—41.7 Revelation 16.1–11	Psalms 121, **122**, 123, 124 or **119.81–104** Isaiah 19 Matthew 10.16–33
Thursday	**26 November**	R/G	Revelation 18.1–2, 21–23; 19.1–3, 9 Psalm 100 Luke 21.20–28	Psalms **125**, 126, 127, 128 or **78.1–39*** Isaiah 41.8–20 Revelation 16.12–end	Psalms 131, 132, **133** or **78.40–end*** Isaiah 21.1–12 Matthew 10.34—11.1
Friday	**27 November**	R/G	Revelation 20.1–4, 11—21.2 Psalm 84.1–6 Luke 21.29–33	Psalms 139 or **55** Isaiah 41.21—42.9 Revelation 17	Psalm **146**, 147 or **69** Isaiah 22.1–14 Matthew 11.2–19
Saturday	**28 November**	R/G	Revelation 22.1–7 Psalm 95.1–7 Luke 21.34–36	Psalm **145** or **76**, 79 Isaiah 42.10–17 Revelation 18	Psalms 148, 149, **150** or 81, **84** Isaiah 24 Matthew 11.20–end

¶ *Additional Weekday Lectionary*

This Additional Weekday Lectionary provides two readings for each day of the year, except for Sundays, Principal Feasts and other Principal Holy Days, Holy Week and Festivals (for which the readings provided in the main body of this lectionary are used). The readings for 'first evensongs' in the main body of the lectionary are used on the eves of Principal Feasts and may be used on the eves of Festivals. This lectionary is intended particularly for use in those places of worship that attract occasional rather than daily worshippers, and can be used either at Morning or Evening Prayer. Psalmody is not provided and should be taken from the daily provision earlier in this volume.

		1 December – Advent 1	
Monday	**2 December**	Malachi 3.1–6	Matthew 3.1–6
Tuesday	**3 December**	Zephaniah 3.14–end	1 Thessalonians 4.13–end
Wednesday	**4 December**	Isaiah 65.17—66.2	Matthew 24.1–14
Thursday	**5 December**	Micah 5.2–5a	John 3.16–21
Friday	**6 December**	Isaiah 66.18–end	Luke 13.22–30
Saturday	**7 December**	Micah 7.8–15	Romans 15.30—16.7, 25–end
		8 December – Advent 2	
Monday	**9 December**	Jeremiah 7.1–11	Philippians 4.4–9
Tuesday	**10 December**	Daniel 7.9–14	Matthew 24.15–28
Wednesday	**11 December**	Amos 9.11–end	Romans 13.8–end
Thursday	**12 December**	Jeremiah 23.5–8	Mark 11.1–11
Friday	**13 December**	Jeremiah 33.14–22	Luke 21.25–36
Saturday	**14 December**	Zechariah 14.4–11	Revelation 22.1–7
		15 December – Advent 3	
Monday	**16 December**	Isaiah 40.1–11	Matthew 3.1–12
Tuesday	**17 December**	Ecclesiasticus 24.1–9 or Proverbs 8.22–31	1 Corinthians 2.1–13
Wednesday	**18 December**	Exodus 3.1–6	Acts 7.20–36
Thursday	**19 December**	Isaiah 11.1–9	Romans 15.7–13
Friday	**20 December**	Isaiah 22.21–23	Revelation 3.7–13
Saturday	**21 December**	Numbers 24.15b–19	Revelation 22.10–21
		22 December – Advent 4	
Monday	**23 December**	Isaiah 7.10–15	Matthew 1.18–23
Tuesday	**24 December**	*At Evening Prayer the readings for Christmas Eve are used. At other services, the following readings are used:* Isaiah 29.13–18	1 John 4.7–16
Wednesday	**25 December**	Christmas Day – see p.13	
Thursday	**26 December**	Stephen, deacon, first martyr – see p.13	
Friday	**27 December**	John, Apostle and Evangelist – see p.13	
Saturday	**28 December**	The Holy Innocents – see p.13	
		29 December – Christmas 1	
Monday	**30 December**	Isaiah 9.2–7	John 8.12–20
Tuesday	**31 December**	Ecclesiastes 3.1–13	Revelation 21.1–8
Wednesday	**1 January**	Naming and Circumcision of Jesus – see p.14	
Thursday	**2 January**	Isaiah 66.6–14	Matthew 12.46–50
Friday	**3 January**	Deuteronomy 6.4–15	John 10.31–end
Saturday	**4 January**	Isaiah 63.7–16	Galatians 3.23—4.7
		If, for pastoral reasons, The Epiphany is celebrated on Sunday 5 January, the readings for the Eve of Epiphany are used at Evening Prayer.	

Monday	6 January	The Epiphany – see p.16	
		or, if, for pastoral reasons, The Epiphany is celebrated on Sunday	
		5 January, the following readings are used:	
		Isaiah 12	2 Corinthians 2.12–end
Tuesday	7 January	Genesis 25.19–end	Ephesians 1.1–6
Wednesday	8 January	Joel 2.28–end	Ephesians 1.7–14
Thursday	9 January	Proverbs 8.12–21	Ephesians 1.15–end
Friday	10 January	Genesis 19.15–29	Ephesians 2.1–10
		At Evening Prayer the readings for the Eve of the Baptism of Christ are used.	
Saturday	11 January	At other services, the following readings are used:	
		Genesis 17.1–14	Ephesians 2.11–end

Monday	13 January	Isaiah 41.14–20	John 1.29–34
Tuesday	14 January	Exodus 17.1–7	Acts 8.26–end
Wednesday	15 January	Exodus 15.1–19	Colossians 2.8–15
Thursday	16 January	Zechariah 6.9–15	1 Peter 2.4–10
Friday	17 January	Isaiah 51.7–16	Galatians 6.14–18
Saturday	18 January	Leviticus 16.11–22	Hebrews 10.19–25

Monday	20 January	1 Kings 17.8–16	Mark 8.1–10
Tuesday	21 January	1 Kings 19.1–9a	Mark 1.9–15
Wednesday	22 January	1 Kings 19.9b–18	Mark 9.2–13
Thursday	23 January	Leviticus 11.1–8, 13–19, 41–45	Acts 10.9–16
Friday	24 January	Isaiah 49.8–13 or 1st EP of the	Acts 10.34–43
		Conversion of Paul	
Saturday	25 January	Conversion of Paul – see p.18	

Monday	27 January	Ezekiel 37.15–end	John 17.1–19
Tuesday	28 January	Ezekiel 20.39–44	John 17.20–end
Wednesday	29 January	Nehemiah 2.1–10	Romans 12.1–8
Thursday	30 January	Deuteronomy 26.16–end	Romans 14.1– 9
Friday	31 January	Leviticus 19.9–28	Romans 15.1–7
Saturday	1 February	At Evening Prayer the readings for the Eve of the Presentation are used.	
		At other services, the following readings are used:	
		Jeremiah 33.1–11	1 Peter 5.5b–end

Monday	3 February	Genesis 1.26–end	Mark 10.1–16
Tuesday	4 February	Ruth 1.1–18	1 John 3.14–end
Wednesday	5 February	1 Samuel 1.19b–end	Luke 2.41–end
Thursday	6 February	Genesis 47.1–12	Ephesians 3.14–end
Friday	7 February	2 Samuel 1.17–end	Romans 8.28–end
Saturday	8 February	Song of Solomon 2.8–end	1 Corinthians 13

Monday	10 February	Exodus 23.1–13	James 2.1–13
Tuesday	11 February	Deuteronomy 10.12–end	Hebrews 13.1–16
Wednesday	12 February	Isaiah 58.6–end	Matthew 25.31–end
Thursday	13 February	Isaiah 42.1–9	Luke 4.14–21
Friday	14 February	Amos 5.6–15	Ephesians 4.25–end
Saturday	15 February	Amos 5.18–24	John 2.13–22

Monday	17 February	Isaiah 61.1–9	Mark 6.1–13
Tuesday	18 February	Isaiah 52.1–10	Romans 10.5–21
Wednesday	19 February	Isaiah 52.13—53.6	Romans 15.14–21
Thursday	20 February	Isaiah 53.4–12	2 Corinthians 4.1–10
Friday	21 February	Zechariah 8.16–end	Matthew 10.1–15
Saturday	22 February	Jeremiah 1.4–10	Matthew 10.16–22

Monday	24 February	2 Kings 2.13–22	3 John
Tuesday	25 February	Judges 14.5–17	Revelation 10.4–11
Wednesday	26 February	Ash Wednesday – see p.23	
Thursday	27 February	Genesis 2.7–end	Hebrews 2.5–end
Friday	28 February	Genesis 4.1–12	Hebrews 4.12–end
Saturday	29 February	2 Kings 22.11–end	Hebrews 5.1–10

1 March – Lent 1

Monday	2 March	Genesis 6.11–end, 7.11–16	Luke 4.14–21
Tuesday	3 March	Deuteronomy 31.7–13	1 John 3.1–10
Wednesday	4 March	Genesis 11.1–9	Matthew 24.15–28
Thursday	5 March	Genesis 13.1–13	1 Peter 2.13–end
Friday	6 March	Genesis 21.1–8	Luke 9.18–27
Saturday	7 March	Genesis 32.22–32	2 Peter 1.10–end

8 March – Lent 2

Monday	9 March	1 Chronicles 21.1–17	1 John 2.1–8
Tuesday	10 March	Zechariah 3	2 Peter 2.1–10a
Wednesday	11 March	Job 1.1–22	Luke 21.34—22.6
Thursday	12 March	2 Chronicles 29.1–11	Mark 11.15–19
Friday	13 March	Exodus 19.1–9a	1 Peter 1.1–9
Saturday	14 March	Exodus 19.9b–19	Acts 7.44–50

15 March – Lent 3

Monday	16 March	Joshua 4.1–13	Luke 9.1–11
Tuesday	17 March	Exodus 15.22–27	Hebrews 10.32–end
Wednesday	18 March	Genesis 9.8–17	1 Peter 3.18–end
		or 1st EP of Joseph of Nazareth	
Thursday	19 March	Joseph of Nazareth – see p.26	
Friday	20 March	Numbers 20.1–13	1 Corinthians 10.23–end
Saturday	21 March	Isaiah 43.14–end	Hebrews 3.1–15

22 March – Lent 4

Monday	23 March	2 Kings 24.18—25.7	1 Corinthians 15.20–34
Tuesday	24 March	At Evening Prayer the readings for the Eve of the Annunciation are used. At other services, the following readings are used:	
		Jeremiah 13.12–19	Acts 13.26–35
Wednesday	25 March	Annunciation of Our Lord to the Blessed Virgin Mary	
Thursday	26 March	Jeremiah 22.11–19	Luke 11.37–52
Friday	27 March	Jeremiah 17.1–14	Luke 6.17–26
Saturday	28 March	Ezra 1	2 Corinthians 1.12–19

29 March – Lent 5

Monday	30 March	Joel 2.12–17	2 John
Tuesday	31 March	Isaiah 58.1–14	Mark 10.32–45
Wednesday	1 April	Job 36.1–12	John 14.1–14
Thursday	2 April	Jeremiah 9.17–22	Luke 13.31–35
Friday	3 April	Lamentations 5.1–3,19–22	John 12.20–26
Saturday	4 April	Job 17.6–end	John 12.27–36

From the Monday of Holy Week until Easter Eve the seasonal lectionary is used: see pp.29–30.

12 April – Easter

Monday	13 April	Isaiah 54.1–14	Romans 1.1–7
Tuesday	14 April	Isaiah 51.1–11	John 5.19–29
Wednesday	15 April	Isaiah 26.1–19	John 20.1–10
Thursday	16 April	Isaiah 43.14–21	Revelation 1.4–end
Friday	17 April	Isaiah 42.10–17	1 Thessalonians 5.1–11
Saturday	18 April	Job 14.1–14	John 21.1–14

19 April – Easter 2

Monday	20 April	Ezekiel 1.22–end	Revelation 4
Tuesday	21 April	Proverbs 8.1–11	Acts 16.6–15
Wednesday	22 April	Hosea 5.15—6.6	I Corinthians 15.1–11
Thursday	23 April	George, Martyr, Patron of England – see p.32	
Friday	24 April	Genesis 6.9–end	I Peter 3.8–end
Saturday	25 April	Mark the Evangelist – see p.32	

26 April – Easter 3

Monday	27 April	Exodus 24.1–11	Revelation 5
Tuesday	28 April	Leviticus 19.9–18, 32–end	Matthew 5.38–end
Wednesday	29 April	Genesis 3.8–21	I Corinthians 15.12–28
Thursday	30 April	Isaiah 33.13–22	Mark 6.47–end
Friday	1 May	Philip and James, Apostles – see p.33	
Saturday	2 May	Isaiah 61.10—62.5	Luke 24.1–12

3 May – Easter 4

Monday	4 May	Jeremiah 31.10–17	Revelation 7.9–end
Tuesday	5 May	Job 31.13–23	Matthew 7.1–12
Wednesday	6 May	Genesis 2.4b–9	I Corinthians 15.35–49
Thursday	7 May	Proverbs 28.3–end	Mark 10.17–31
Friday	8 May	Ecclesiastes 12.1–8	Romans 6.1–11
Saturday	9 May	I Chronicles 29.10–13	Luke 24.13–35

10 May – Easter 5

Monday	11 May	Genesis 15.1–18	Romans 4.13–end
Tuesday	12 May	Deuteronomy 8.1–10	Matthew 6.19–end
Wednesday	13 May	Hosea 13.4–14	I Corinthians 15.50–end
Thursday	14 May	Matthias the Apostle – see p.35	
Friday	15 May	Ezekiel 36.33–end	Romans 8.1–11
Saturday	16 May	Isaiah 38.9–20	Luke 24.33–end

17 May – Easter 6

Monday	18 May	Proverbs 4.1–13	Philippians 2.1–11
Tuesday	19 May	Isaiah 32.12–end	Romans 5.1–11
Wednesday	20 May	At Evening Prayer the readings for the Eve of Ascension Day are used.	
		At other services, the following readings are used:	
		Isaiah 43.1–13	Titus 2.11—3.8
Thursday	21 May	Ascension Day – see p.37	
Friday	22 May	Exodus 35.30—36.1	Galatians 5.13–end
Saturday	23 May	Numbers 11.16–17, 24–29	I Corinthians 2

24 May – Easter 7

Monday	25 May	Numbers 27.15–end	I Corinthians 3
Tuesday	26 May	I Samuel 10.1–10	I Corinthians 12.1–13
Wednesday	27 May	I Kings 19.1–18	Matthew 3.13–end
Thursday	28 May	Ezekiel 11.14–20	Matthew 9.35—10.20
Friday	29 May	Ezekiel 36.22–28	Matthew 12.22–32
Saturday	30 May	At Evening Prayer the readings for the Eve of Pentecost are used.	
		At other services, the following readings are used:	
		Micah 3.1–8	Ephesians 6.10–20

31 May – Pentecost

Monday	1 June	The Visit of the Blessed Virgin Mary to Elizabeth (transferred from 31 May) – see p.39	
Tuesday	2 June	Genesis 13.1–12	Romans 12.9–end
Wednesday	3 June	Genesis 15	Romans 4.1–8
Thursday	4 June	Genesis 22.1–18	Hebrews 11.8–19
Friday	5 June	Isaiah 51.1–8	John 8.48–end
Saturday	6 June	At Evening Prayer the readings for the Eve of Trinity Sunday are used.	
		At other services, the following readings are used:	
		Ecclesiasticus 44.19–23 or	
		Joshua 2.1–15	James 2.14–26

Monday	8 June	Exodus 2.1–10	Hebrews 11.23–31
Tuesday	9 June	Exodus 2.11–end	Acts 7.17–29
Wednesday	10 June	Exodus 3.1–12	Acts 7.30–38
		or 1st EP of Corpus Christi	
		or 1st EP of Barnabas the Apostle	
Thursday	11 June	Day of Thanksgiving for the Institution of Holy Communion	
		(Corpus Christi) – see p.41	
		or, where Corpus Christi *is not celebrated as a Festival:*	
		Barnabas the Apostle – see p.42	
Friday	12 June	*Where* Corpus Christi *is celebrated as a Festival on 11 June:*	
		Barnabas the Apostle – see p.41	
		or, where Corpus Christi *is not celebrated as a Festival:*	
		Exodus 34.1–10	Mark 7.1–13
Saturday	13 June	Exodus 34.27–end	2 Corinthians 3.7–end

Monday	15 June	Genesis 37.1–11	Romans 12.9–21
Tuesday	16 June	Genesis 41.15–40	Mark 13.1–13
Wednesday	17 June	Genesis 42.17–end	Matthew 18.1–14
Thursday	18 June	Genesis 45.1–15	Acts 7.9–16
Friday	19 June	Genesis 47.1–12	1 Thessalonians 5.12–end
Saturday	20 June	Genesis 50.4–21	Luke 15.11–end

Monday	22 June	Isaiah 32	James 3.13–end
Tuesday	23 June	Proverbs 3.1–18	Matthew 5.1–12
		or 1st EP of Birth of John the Baptist	
Wednesday	24 June	Birth of John the Baptist – see p.44	
Thursday	25 June	Jeremiah 6.9–15	1 Timothy 2.1–6
Friday	26 June	1 Samuel 16.14–end	John 14.15–end
Saturday	27 June	Isaiah 6.1–9	Revelation 19.9–end

Monday	29 June	Peter and Paul, Apostles, *or* Peter the Apostle – see p.45	
Tuesday	30 June	Proverbs 1.20–end	James 5.13–end
Wednesday	1 July	Isaiah 5.8–24	James 1.17–25
Thursday	2 July	Isaiah 57.14–end	John 13.1–17
		or 1st EP of Thomas the Apostle	
Friday	3 July	Thomas the Apostle – see p.45	
Saturday	4 July	Isaiah 25.1–9	Acts 2.22–33

Monday	6 July	Exodus 20.1–17	Matthew 6.1–15
Tuesday	7 July	Proverbs 6.6–19	Luke 4.1–14
Wednesday	8 July	Isaiah 24.1–15	1 Corinthians 6.1–11
Thursday	9 July	Job 7	Matthew 7.21–29
Friday	10 July	Jeremiah 20.7–end	Matthew 27.27–44
Saturday	11 July	Job 28	Hebrews 11.32—12.2

Monday	13 July	Exodus 32.1–14	Colossians 3.1–11
Tuesday	14 July	Proverbs 9.1–12	2 Thessalonians 2.13—3.5
Wednesday	15 July	Isaiah 26.1–9	Romans 8.12–27
Thursday	16 July	Jeremiah 8.18—9.6	John 13.21–35
Friday	17 July	2 Samuel 5.1–12	Matthew 27.45–56
Saturday	18 July	Hosea 11.1–11	Matthew 28.1–7

Monday	20 July	Exodus 40.1–16	Luke 14.15–24
Tuesday	21 July	Proverbs 11.1–12	Mark 12.38–44
		or 1st EP of Mary Magdalene	
Wednesday	22 July	Mary Magdalene – see p.48	
Thursday	23 July	Job 38	Luke 18.1–14
Friday	24 July	Job 42.1–6	John 3.1–15
		or 1st EP of James the Apostle	
Saturday	25 July	James the Apostle – see p.48	

Monday	27 July	Numbers 23.1–12	1 Corinthians 1.10–17
Tuesday	28 July	Proverbs 12.1–12	Galatians 3.1–14
Wednesday	29 July	Isaiah 49.8–13	2 Corinthians 8.1–11
Thursday	30 July	Hosea 14	John 15.1–17
Friday	31 July	2 Samuel 18.18–end	Matthew 27.57–66
Saturday	1 August	Isaiah 55.1–7	Mark 16.1–8

Monday	3 August	Joel 3.16–21	Mark 4.21–34
Tuesday	4 August	Proverbs 12.13–end	John 1.43–51
Wednesday	5 August	Isaiah 55.8–end	2 Timothy 2.8–19
		or 1st EP of Transfiguration of Our Lord	
Thursday	6 August	Transfiguration of Our Lord – see p.50	
Friday	7 August	Jeremiah 14.1–9	Luke 8.4–15
Saturday	8 August	Ecclesiastes 5.10–19	1 Timothy 6.6–16

Monday	10 August	Joshua 1.1–9	1 Corinthians 9.19–end
Tuesday	11 August	Proverbs 15.1–11	Galatians 2.15–end
Wednesday	12 August	Isaiah 49.1–7	1 John 1
Thursday	13 August	Proverbs 27.1–12	John 15.12–27
Friday	14 August	Isaiah 59.8–end	Mark 15.6–20
		or 1st EP of The Blessed Virgin Mary	
Saturday	15 August	The Blessed Virgin Mary – see p.51	

Monday	17 August	Judges 13.1–23	Luke 10.38–42
Tuesday	18 August	Proverbs 15.15–end	Matthew 15.21–28
Wednesday	19 August	Isaiah 45.1–7	Ephesians 4.1–16
Thursday	20 August	Jeremiah 16.1–15	Luke 12.35–48
Friday	21 August	Jeremiah 18.1–11	Hebrews 1.1–9
Saturday	22 August	Jeremiah 26.1–19	Ephesians 3.1–13

Monday	24 August	Bartholomew the Apostle – see p.53	
Tuesday	25 August	Proverbs 16.1–11	Philippians 3.4b–end
Wednesday	26 August	Deuteronomy 11.1–21	2 Corinthians 9.6–end
Thursday	27 August	Ecclesiasticus 2	John 16.1–15
		or Ecclesiastes 2.12–25	
Friday	28 August	Obadiah 1–10	John 19.1–16
Saturday	29 August	2 Kings 2.11–14	Luke 24.36–end

Monday	31 August	1 Samuel 17.32–50	Matthew 8.14–22
Tuesday	1 September	Proverbs 17.1–15	Luke 7.1–17
Wednesday	2 September	Jeremiah 5.20–end	2 Peter 3.8–end
Thursday	3 September	Daniel 2.1–23	Luke 10.1–20
Friday	4 September	Daniel 3.1–28	Revelation 15
Saturday	5 September	Daniel 6	Philippians 2.14–24

Monday	7 September	2 Samuel 7.4–17	2 Corinthians 5.1–10
Tuesday	8 September	Proverbs 18.10–21	Romans 14.10–end
Wednesday	9 September	Judges 4.1–10	Romans 1.8–17
Thursday	10 September	Isaiah 49.14–end	John 16.16–24
Friday	11 September	Job 9.1–24	Mark 15.21–32
Saturday	12 September	Exodus 19.1–9	John 20.11–18

Monday	**14 September**	Holy Cross Day – see p.56	
Tuesday	**15 September**	Proverbs 21.1–18	Mark 6.30–44
Wednesday	**16 September**	Hosea 11.1–11	1 John 4.9–end
Thursday	**17 September**	Lamentations 3.34–48	Romans 7.14–end
Friday	**18 September**	1 Kings 19.4–18	1 Thessalonians 3
Saturday	**19 September**	Ecclesiasticus 4.11–28	2 Timothy 3.10–end
		or Deuteronomy 29.2–15	

Monday	**21 September**	Matthew, Apostle and Evangelist – see p.57	
Tuesday	**22 September**	Proverbs 8.1–11	Luke 6.39–end
Wednesday	**23 September**	Proverbs 2.1–15	Colossians 1.9–20
Thursday	**24 September**	Baruch 3.14–end	John 1.1–18
		or Genesis 1.1–13	
Friday	**25 September**	Ecclesiasticus 1.1–20	1 Corinthians 1.18–end
		or Deuteronomy 7.7–16	
Saturday	**26 September**	Wisdom 9.1–12	Luke 2.41–end
		or Jeremiah 1.4–10	

Monday	**28 September**	Genesis 21.1–13	Luke 1.26–38
		or 1st EP of Michael and All Angels	
Tuesday	**29 September**	Michael and All Angels – see p.58	
Wednesday	**30 September**	2 Kings 4.1–7	John 2.1–11
Thursday	**1 October**	2 Kings 4.25b–37	Mark 3.19b–35
Friday	**2 October**	Judith 8.9–17, 28–36	John 19.25b–30
		or Ruth 1.1–18	
Saturday	**3 October**	Exodus 15.19–27	Acts 1.6–14

Monday	**5 October**	Exodus 19.16–end	Hebrews 12.18–end
Tuesday	**6 October**	1 Chronicles 16.1–13	Revelation 11.15–end
Wednesday	**7 October**	1 Chronicles 29.10–19	Colossians 3.12–17
Thursday	**8 October**	Nehemiah 8.1–12	1 Corinthians 14.1–12
Friday	**9 October**	Isaiah 1.10–17	Mark 12.28–34
Saturday	**10 October**	Daniel 6.6–23	Revelation 12.7–12

Monday	**12 October**	2 Samuel 22.4–7, 17–20	Hebrews 7.26—8.6
Tuesday	**13 October**	Proverbs 22.17–end	2 Corinthians 12.1–10
Wednesday	**14 October**	Hosea 14	James 2.14–26
Thursday	**15 October**	Isaiah 24.1–15	John 16.25–33
Friday	**16 October**	Jeremiah 14.1–9	Luke 23.44–56
Saturday	**17 October**	Zechariah 8.14–end	John 20.19–end
		or 1st EP of Luke the Evangelist	

Monday	**19 October**	1 Kings 3.3–14	1 Timothy 3.14–4.8
		or Luke the Evangelist transferred – see p.61	
Tuesday	**20 October**	Proverbs 27.11–end	Galatians 6.1–10
Wednesday	**21 October**	Isaiah 51.1–6	2 Corinthians 1.1–11
Thursday	**22 October**	Ecclesiasticus 18.1–14	1 Corinthians 11.17–end
		or Job 26	
Friday	**23 October**	Ecclesiasticus 28.2–12	Mark 15.33–47
		or Job 19.21–end	
Saturday	**24 October**	Isaiah 44.21–end	John 21.15–end

Monday	26 October	Isaiah 42.14–21	Luke 1.5–25
Tuesday	27 October	1 Samuel 4.12–end	Luke 1.57–80
		or 1st EP of Simon and Jude, Apostles	
Wednesday	28 October	Simon and Jude, Apostles – see p.64	
Thursday	29 October	Isaiah 35	Matthew 11.2–19
Friday	30 October	2 Samuel 11.1–17	Matthew 14.1–12
Saturday	31 October	At Evening Prayer the readings for the Eve of All Saints' Day are used.	
		At other services, the following readings are used:	
		Isaiah 43.15–21	Acts 19.1–10

Monday	2 November	Esther 3.1–11, 4.7–17	Matthew 18.1–10
Tuesday	3 November	Ezekiel 18.21–end	Matthew 18.12–20
Wednesday	4 November	Proverbs 3.27–end	Matthew 18.21–end
Thursday	5 November	Exodus 23.1–9	Matthew 19.1–15
Friday	6 November	Proverbs 3.13–18	Matthew 19.16–end
Saturday	7 November	Deuteronomy 28.1–6	Matthew 20.1–16

Monday	9 November	Isaiah 40.21–end	Romans 11.25–end
Tuesday	10 November	Ezekiel 34.20–end	John 10.1–18
Wednesday	11 November	Leviticus 26.3–13	Titus 2.1–10
Thursday	12 November	Hosea 6.1–6	Matthew 9.9–13
Friday	13 November	Malachi 4	John 4.5–26
Saturday	14 November	Micah 6.6–8	Colossians 3.12–17

Monday	16 November	Micah 7.1–7	Matthew 10.24–39
Tuesday	17 November	Habakkuk 3.1–19a	1 Corinthians 4.9–16
Wednesday	18 November	Zechariah 8.1–13	Mark 13.3–8
Thursday	19 November	Zechariah 10.6–end	1 Peter 5.1–11
Friday	20 November	Micah 4.1–5	Luke 9.28–36
Saturday	21 November	At Evening Prayer the readings for the Eve of Christ the King are used.	
		At other services, the following readings are used:	
		Exodus 16.1–21	John 6.3–15

Monday	23 November	Jeremiah 30.1–3, 10–17	Romans 12.9–21
Tuesday	24 November	Jeremiah 30.18–24	John 10.22–30
Wednesday	25 November	Jeremiah 31.1–9	Matthew 15.21–31
Thursday	26 November	Jeremiah 31.10–17	Matthew 16.13–end
Friday	27 November	Jeremiah 31.31–37	Hebrews 10.11–18
Saturday	28 November	Isaiah 51.17—52.2	Ephesians 5.1–20

¶ *Collects and Post Communions*

All the contemporary language Collects and Post Communions, including the Additional Collects, may be found in *Common Worship: Collects and Post Communions* (Church House Publishing: London, 2004). The Additional Collects are also published separately.

The contemporary language Collects and Post Communions all appear in *Times and Seasons: President's Edition for Holy Communion*. Apart from the Additional Collects, they appear in the other Common Worship volumes as follows:

¶ President's edition: all Collects and Post Communions;
¶ *Daily Prayer*: all Collects;
¶ main volume: Collects and Post Communions for Sundays, Principal Feasts and Holy Days, and Festivals;
¶ *Festivals*: Collects and Post Communions for Festivals, Lesser Festivals, Common of the Saints and Special Occasions.

The traditional-language Collects and Post Communions all appear in the president's edition. They appear in other publications as follows:

¶ main volume: Collects and Post Communions for Sundays, Principal Feasts and Holy Days, and Festivals;
¶ separate booklet: Collects and Post Communions for Lesser Festivals, Common of the Saints and Special Occasions.

¶ *Lectionary for Dedication Festival*

If date not known, observe on the first Sunday in October or Last Sunday after Trinity.

Evening Prayer on the Eve
Psalm 24
2 Chronicles 7.11–16
John 4.19–29

Dedication Festival
Gold or White

	Principal Service	3rd Service	2nd Service	Psalmody
Year A	1 Kings 8.22–30 *or* Revelation 21.9–14 Psalm 122 Hebrews 12.18–24 Matthew 21.12–16	Haggai 2.6–9 Hebrews 10.19–25	Jeremiah 7.1–11 1 Corinthians 3.9–17 *HC* Luke 19.1–10	*MP* 48, 150 *EP* 132
Year B	Genesis 28.11–18 *or* Revelation 21.9–14 Psalm 122 1 Peter 2.1–10 John 10.22–29	Haggai 2.6–9 Hebrews 10.19–25	Jeremiah 7.1–11 Luke 19.1–10	*MP* 48, 150 *EP* 132
Year C	1 Chronicles 29.6–19 Psalm 122 Ephesians 2.19–22 John 2.13–22	Haggai 2.6–9 Hebrews 10.19–25	Jeremiah 7.1–11 Luke 19.1–10	*MP* 48, 150 *EP* 132

The Blessed Virgin Mary

Genesis 3.8–15, 20; Isaiah 7.10–14; Micah 5.1–4
Psalms 45.10–17; 113; 131
Acts 1.12–14; Romans 8.18–30; Galatians 4.4–7
Luke 1.26–38; *or* 1.39–47; John 19.25–27

Martyrs

2 Chronicles 24.17–21; Isaiah 43.1–7; Jeremiah 11.18–20; Wisdom 4.10–15
Psalms 3; 11; 31.1–5; 44.18–24; 126
Romans 8.35–end; 2 Corinthians 4.7–15; 2 Timothy 2.3–7 [8–13]; Hebrews 11.32–end;
    1 Peter 4.12–end; Revelation 12.10–12a
Matthew 10.16–22; *or* 10.28–39; *or* 16.24–26; John 12.24–26; *or* 15.18–21

Agnes (21 Jan): *also* Revelation 7.13–end
Alban (22 June): *especially* 2 Timothy 2.3–13; John 12.24–26
Alphege (19 Apr): *also* Hebrews 5.1–4
Boniface (5 June): *also* Acts 20.24–28
Charles (30 Jan): *also* Ecclesiasticus 2.12–end; 1 Timothy 6.12–16
Clement (23 Nov): *also* Philippians 3.17—4.3; Matthew 16.13–19
Cyprian (15 Sept): *especially* 1 Peter 4.12–end; *also* Matthew 18.18–22
Edmund (20 Nov): *also* Proverbs 20.28; 21.1–4, 7
Ignatius (17 Oct): *also* Philippians 3.7–12; John 6.52–58
James Hannington (29 Oct): *especially* Matthew 10.28–39
Janani Luwum (17 Feb): *also* Ecclesiasticus 4.20–28; John 12.24–32
John Coleridge Patteson (20 Sept): *especially* 2 Chronicles 24.17–21; *also* Acts 7.55–end
Justin (1 June): *especially* John 15.18–21; *also* 1 Maccabees 2.15–22; 1 Corinthians 1.18–25
Laurence (10 Aug): *also* 2 Corinthians 9.6–10
Lucy (13 Dec): *also* Wisdom 3.1–7; 2 Corinthians 4.6–15
Oswald (5 Aug): *especially* 1 Peter 4.12–end; John 16.29–end
Perpetua, Felicity and comps (7 Mar): *especially* Revelation 12.10–12a; *also* Wisdom 3.1–7
Polycarp (23 Feb): *also* Revelation 2.8–11
Thomas Becket (29 Dec *or* 7 Jul): *especially* Matthew 10.28–33; *also* Ecclesiasticus 51.1–8
William Tyndale (6 Oct): *also* Proverbs 8.4–11; 2 Timothy 3.12–end

Teachers of the Faith and Spiritual Writers

1 Kings 3.[6–10] 11–14; Proverbs 4.1–9; Wisdom 7.7–10, 15–16; Ecclesiasticus 39.1–10
Psalms 19.7–10; 34.11–17; 37.31–35; 119.89–96; 119.97–104
1 Corinthians 1.18–25; *or* 2.1–10; *or* 2.9–end; Ephesians 3.8–12; 2 Timothy 4.1–8;
    Titus 2.1–8
Matthew 5.13–19; *or* 13.52–end; *or* 23.8–12; Mark 4.1–9; John 16.12–15

Ambrose (7 Dec): *also* Isaiah 41.9*b*–13; Luke 22.24–30
Anselm (21 Apr): *also* Wisdom 9.13–end; Romans 5.8–11
Athanasius (2 May): *also* Ecclesiasticus 4.20–28; *also* Matthew 10.24–27
Augustine of Hippo (28 Aug): *especially* Ecclesiasticus 39.1–10; *also* Romans 13.11–13
Basil and Gregory (2 Jan): *especially* 2 Timothy 4.1–8; Matthew 5.13–19
Bernard (20 Aug): *especially* Revelation 19.5–9
Catherine of Siena (29 Apr): *also* Proverbs 8.1, 6–11; John 17.12–end
Francis de Sales (24 Jan): *also* Proverbs 3.13–18; John 3.17–21
Gregory the Great (3 Sept): *also* 1 Thessalonians 2.3–8
Gregory of Nyssa and Macrina (19 July): *especially* 1 Corinthians 2.9–13;
    also Wisdom 9.13–17
Hilary (13 Jan): *also* 1 John 2.18–25; John 8.25–32
Irenaeus (28 June): *also* 2 Peter 1.16–end
Jeremy Taylor (13 Aug); *also* Titus 2.7–8, 11–14
John Bunyan (30 Aug): *also* Hebrews 12.1–2; Luke 21.21, 34–36
John Chrysostom (13 Sept): *especially* Matthew 5.13–19; *also* Jeremiah 1.4–10
John of the Cross (14 Dec): *especially* 1 Corinthians 2.1–10; *also* John 14.18–23
Leo (10 Nov): *also* 1 Peter 5.1–11
Richard Hooker (3 Nov): *especially* John 16.12–15; *also* Ecclesiasticus 44.10–15
Teresa of Avila (15 Oct): *also* Romans 8.22–27
Thomas Aquinas (28 Jan): *especially* Wisdom 7.7–10, 15–16; 1 Corinthians 2.9–end;
    John 16.12–15
William Law (10 Apr): *especially* 1 Corinthians 2.9–end; *also* Matthew 17.1–9

Bishops and Other Pastors

I Samuel 16.1, 6–13; Isaiah 6.1–8; Jeremiah 1.4–10; Ezekiel 3.16–21; Malachi 2.5–7
Psalms 1; 15; 16.5–end; 96; 110
Acts 20.28–35; 1 Corinthians 4.1–5; 2 Corinthians 4.1–10 [or 1–2, 5–7];
    or 5.14–20; 1 Peter 5.1–4
Matthew 11.25–end; or 24.42–46; John 10.11–16; or 15.9–17; or 21.15–17

Augustine of Canterbury (26 May): also 1 Thessalonians 2.2b–8; Matthew 13.31–33
Charles Simeon (13 Nov): especially Malachi 2.5–7; also Colossians 1.3–8; Luke 8.4–8
David (1 Mar): also 2 Samuel 23.1–4; Psalm 89.19–22, 24
Dunstan (19 May): especially Matthew 24.42–46; also Exodus 31.1–5
Edward King (8 Mar): also Hebrews 13.1–8
George Herbert (27 Feb): especially Malachi 2.5–7; Matthew 11.25–end;
    also Revelation 19.5–9
Hugh (17 Nov); also 1 Timothy 6.11–16
John Keble (14 July): also Lamentations 3.19–26; Matthew 5.1–8
John and Charles Wesley (24 May): also Ephesians 5.15–20
Lancelot Andrewes (25 Sept): especially Isaiah 6.1–8
Martin of Tours (11 Nov): also 1 Thessalonians 5.1–11; Matthew 25.34–40
Nicholas (6 Dec): also Isaiah 61.1–3; 1 Timothy 6.6–11; Mark 10.13–16
Richard (16 June): also John 21.15–19
Swithun (15 July): also James 5.7–11, 13–18
Thomas Ken (8 June): especially 2 Corinthians 4.1–10 [or 1–2, 5–7]; Matthew 24.42–46
Wulfstan (19 Jan): especially Matthew 24.42–46

Members of Religious Communities

I Kings 19.9–18; Proverbs 10.27–end; Song of Solomon 8.6–7; Isaiah 61.10—62.5;
Hosea 2.14–15, 19–20
Psalms 34.1–8; 112.1–9; 119.57–64; 123; 131
Acts 4.32–35; 2 Corinthians 10.17—11.2; Philippians 3.7–14; I John 2.15–17;
Revelation 19.1, 5–9
Matthew 11.25–end; or 19.3–12; or 19.23–end; Luke 9.57–end; or 12.32–37

Aelred (12 Jan): also Ecclesiasticus 15.1–6
Alcuin (20 May): also Colossians 3.12–16; John 4.19–24
Antony (17 Jan): especially Philippians 3.7–14, also Matthew 19.16–26
Bede (25 May): also Ecclesiasticus 39.1–10
Benedict (11 July): also I Corinthians 3.10–11; Luke 18.18–22
Clare (11 Aug): especially Song of Solomon 8.6–7
Dominic (8 Aug): also Ecclesiasticus 39.1–10
Etheldreda (23 June): also Matthew 25.1–13
Francis of Assisi (4 Oct): also Galatians 6.14–end; Luke 12.22–34
Hilda (19 Nov): especially Isaiah 61.10—62.5
Hildegard (17 Sept): also I Corinthians 2.9–13; Luke 10.21–24
Julian of Norwich (8 May): also I Corinthians 13.8–end; Matthew 5.13–16
Vincent de Paul (27 Sept): also I Corinthians 1.25–end; Matthew 25.34–40

Missionaries

Isaiah 52.7–10; or 61.1–3a; Ezekiel 34.11–16; Jonah 3.1–5
Psalms 67; or 87; or 97; or 100; or 117
Acts 2.14, 22–36; or 13.46–49; or 16.6–10; or 26.19–23; Romans 15.17–21;
2 Corinthians 5.11—6.2
Matthew 9.35–end; or 28.16–end; Mark 16.15–20; Luke 5.1–11; or 10.1–9

Aidan (31 Aug): also I Corinthians 9.16–19
Anskar (3 Feb): especially Isaiah 52.7–10; also Romans 10.11–15
Chad (2 Mar or 26 Oct): also I Timothy 6.11b–16
Columba (9 June): also Titus 2.11–end
Cuthbert (20 Mar or 4 Sept): especially Ezekiel 34.11–16; also Matthew 18.12–14
Cyril and Methodius (14 Feb): especially Isaiah 52.7–10; also Romans 10.11–15
Henry Martyn (19 Oct): especially Mark 16.15–end; also Isaiah 55.6–11
Ninian (16 Sept): especially Acts 13.46–49; Mark 16.15–end
Patrick (17 Mar): also Psalm 91.1–4, 13–end; Luke 10.1–12, 17–20
Paulinus (10 Oct); especially Matthew 28.16–end
Wilfrid (12 Oct): especially Luke 5.1–11; also I Corinthians 1.18–25
Willibrord (7 Nov): especially Isaiah 52.7–10; Matthew 28.16–end

Any Saint

General

Genesis 12.1–4; Proverbs 8.1–11; Micah 6.6–8; Ecclesiasticus 2.7–13 [14–end]
Psalms 32; 33.1–5; 119.1–8; 139.1–4 [5–12]; 145.8–14
Ephesians 3.14–19; *or* 6.11–18; Hebrews 13.7–8, 15–16; James 2.14–17;
   1 John 4.7–16; Revelation 21.[1–4] 5–7
Matthew 19.16–21; *or* 25.1–13; *or* 25.14–30; John 15.1–8; *or* 17.20–end

Christian rulers

1 Samuel 16.1–13*a*; 1 Kings 3.3–14
Psalms 72.1–7; 99
1 Timothy 2.1–6
Mark 10.42–45; Luke 14.27–33

Alfred the Great (26 Oct): *also* 2 Samuel 23.1–5; John 18.33–37
Edward the Confessor (13 Oct): *also* 2 Samuel 23.1–5; 1 John 4.13–16
Margaret of Scotland (16 Nov): *also* Proverbs 31.10–12, 20, 26–end;
   1 Corinthians 12.13—13.3; Matthew 25.34–end

Those working for the poor and underprivileged

Isaiah 58.6–11
Psalms 82; 146.5–10
Hebrews 13.1–3; 1 John 3.14–18
Matthew 5.1–12; *or* 25.31–end

Elizabeth of Hungary (18 Nov): *especially* Matthew 25.31–end; *also* Proverbs 31.10–end
Josephine Butler (30 May): *especially* Isaiah 58.6–11; *also* 1 John 3.18–23; Matthew 9.10–13
William Wilberforce, Olaudah Equiano and Thomas Clarkson (30 July): *also* Job 31.16–23;
   Galatians 3.26–end, 4.6–7; Luke 4.16–21

Men and women of learning

Proverbs 8.22–31; Ecclesiasticus 44.1–15
Psalms 36.5–10; 49.1–4
Philippians 4.7–8
Matthew 13.44–46, 52; John 7.14–18

Those whose holiness was revealed in marriage and family life

Proverbs 31.10–13, 19–20, 30–end; Tobit 8.4–7
Psalms 127; 128
1 Peter 3.1–9
Mark 3.31–end; Luke 10.38–end

Mary Sumner (9 Aug): *also* Hebrews 13.1–5
Monica (27 Aug): *also* Ecclesiasticus 26.1–3, 13–16

The Guidance of the Holy Spirit

Proverbs 24.3–7; Isaiah 30.15–21; Wisdom 9.13–17
Psalms 25.1–9; 104.26–33; 143.8–10
Acts 15.23–29; Romans 8:22–27; 1 Corinthians 12.4–13
Luke 14.27–33; John 14.23–26; *or* 16.13–15

Rogation Days
(18–20 May in 2020)

Deuteronomy 8.1–10; 1 Kings 8.35–40; Job 28.1–11
Psalms 104.21–30; 107.1–9; 121
Philippians 4.4–7; 2 Thessalonians 3.6–13; 1 John 5.12–15
Matthew 6.1–15; Mark 11.22–24; Luke 11.5–13

Harvest Thanksgiving

Year A	**Year B**	**Year C**
Deuteronomy 8.7–18 *or* 28.1–14	Joel 2.21–27	Deuteronomy 26.1–11
Psalm 65	Psalm 126	Psalm 100
2 Corinthians 9.6–end	1 Timothy 2.1–7; *or* 6.6–10	Philippians 4.4–9
Luke 12.16–30; *or* 17.11–19	Matthew 6.25–33	*or* Revelation 14.14–18
		John 6.25–35

Mission and Evangelism

Isaiah 49.1–6; *or* 52.7–10; Micah 4.1–5
Psalms 2; 46; 67
Acts 17.10–end; 2 Corinthians 5.14—6.2; Ephesians 2.13–end
Matthew 5.13–16; *or* 28.16–end; John 17.20–end

The Unity of the Church

Jeremiah 33.6–9*a*; Ezekiel 36.23–28; Zephaniah 3.16–end
Psalms 100; 122; 133
Ephesians 4.1–6; Colossians 3.9–17; 1 John 4.9–15
Matthew 18.19–22; John 11.45–52; *or* 17.11*b*–23

The Peace of the World

Isaiah 9.1–6; *or* 57.15–19; Micah 4.1–5
Psalms 40.14–17; 72.1–7; 85.8–13
Philippians 4.6–9; 1 Timothy 2.1–6; James 3.13–18
Matthew 5.43–end; John 14.23–29; *or* 15.9–17

Social Justice and Responsibility

Isaiah 32.15–end; Amos 5.21–24; *or* 8.4–7; Acts 5.1–11
Psalms 31.21–24; 85.1–7; 146.5–10
Colossians 3.12–15; James 2.1–4
Matthew 5.1–12; *or* 25.31–end; Luke 16.19–end

Ministry, including Ember Days
(See page 7)

Numbers 11.16–17, 24–29; *or* 27.15–end; 1 Samuel 16.1–13*a*; Isaiah 6.1–8;
    or 61.1–3; Jeremiah 1.4–10
Psalms 40.8–13; 84.8–12; 89.19–25; 101.1–5, 7; 122
Acts 20.28–35; 1 Corinthians 3.3–11; Ephesians 4.4–16; Philippians 3.7–14
Luke 4.16–21; *or* 12.35–43; *or* 22.24–27; John 4.31–38; *or* 15.5–17

In Time of Trouble

Genesis 9.8–17; Job 1.13–end; Isaiah 38.6–11
Psalms 86.1–7; 107.4–15; 142.1–7
Romans 3.21–26; Romans 8.18–25; 2 Corinthians 8.1–5, 9
Mark 4.35–end; Luke 12.1–7; John 16.31–end

For the Sovereign

Joshua 1.1–9; Proverbs 8.1–16
Psalms 20; 101; 121
Romans 13.1–10; Revelation 21.22—22.4
Matthew 22.16–22; Luke 22.24–30

The anniversary of HM The Queen's accession is 6 February.

¶ *Psalms in the Course of a Month*

The following provision may be used for a monthly cycle of psalmody in place of the psalms provided in the tables in this booklet. It is based on the provision in The Book of Common Prayer.

	Morning Prayer	**Evening Prayer**
1	1—5	6—8
2	9—11	12—14
3	15—17	18
4	19—21	22—23
5	24—26	27—29
6	30—31	32—34
7	35—36	37
8	38—40	41—43
9	44—46	47—49
10	50—52	53—55
11	56—58	59—61
12	62—64	65—67
13	68	69—70
14	71—72	73—74
15	75—77	78
16	79—81	82—85
17	86—88	89
18	90—92	93—94
19	95—97	98—101
20	102—103	104
21	105	106
22	107	108—109
23	110—112	113—115
24	116—118	119.1–32
25	119.33–72	119.73–96
26	119.97–144	119.145–176
27	120—125	126—131
28	132—135	136—138
29	139—140	141—143
30	144—146	147—150

In February the psalms are read only to the 28th or 29th day of the month.

In January, March, May, July, August, October and December, all of which have 31 days, the same psalms are read on the last day of the month (being an ordinary weekday) which were read the day before, or else the psalms of the monthly course omitted on one of the Sundays in that month.

Concise Calendar November 2020 – December 2021

Advent 2020 to the eve of Advent 2021: Year B (Daily Eucharistic Lectionary Year 1)

November 2020

Sunday	AllSs	3bAdv	2bAdv	ChrK	Adv1
Monday	2	9	16	23	30
Tuesday	3	10	17	24	
Wednesday	4	11	18	25	
Thursday	5	12	19	26	
Friday	6	13	20	27	
Saturday	7	14	21	28	

December 2020

Sunday		Adv2	Adv3	Adv4	Chr1
Monday		7	14	21	28
Tuesday	1	8	15	22	29
Wednesday	2	9	16	23	30
Thursday	3	10	17	24	31
Friday	4	11	18	Chr	
Saturday	5	12	19	26	

January 2021

Sunday		Chr2	Bapt	Ep2	Ep3	Ep4
Monday		4	11	18	25	
Tuesday		5	12	19	26	
Wednesday		Epiph	13	20	27	
Thursday		7	14	21	28	
Friday	1	8	15	22	29	
Saturday	2	9	16	23	30	

February 2021

Sunday		2bLnt	NbLnt	Lnt1	Lnt2
Monday	1	8	15	22	
Tuesday	Pres	9	16	23	
Wednesday	3	10	Ash W	24	
Thursday	4	11	18	25	
Friday	5	12	19	26	
Saturday	6	13	20	27	

March 2021

Sunday		Lnt3	Lnt4	Lnt5	PmS
Monday	1	8	15	22	29
Tuesday	2	9	16	23	30
Wednesday	3	10	17	24	31
Thursday	4	11	18	Ann	
Friday	5	12	19	26	
Saturday	6	13	20	27	

April 2021

Sunday		Est	Est2	Est3	Est4
Monday		5	12	19	26
Tuesday		6	13	20	27
Wednesday		7	14	21	28
Thursday	1	8	15	22	29
Friday	2	9	16	23	30
Saturday	3	10	17	24	

May 2021

Sunday		Est5	Est6	Est7	Pent	TrS
Monday		3	10	17	24	31
Tuesday		4	11	18	25	
Wednesday		5	12	19	26	
Thursday		6	Ascn	20	27	
Friday		7	14	21	28	
Saturday	1	8	15	22	29	

June 2021

Sunday		Tr1	Tr2	Tr3	Tr4
Monday		7	14	21	28
Tuesday	1	8	15	22	29
Wednesday	2	9	16	23	30
Thursday	3	10	17	24	
Friday	4	11	18	25	
Saturday	5	12	19	26	

July 2021

Sunday		Tr5	Tr6	Tr7	Tr8
Monday		5	12	19	26
Tuesday		6	13	20	27
Wednesday		7	14	21	28
Thursday	1	8	15	22	29
Friday	2	9	16	23	30
Saturday	3	10	17	24	31

August 2021

Sunday	Tr9	Tr10	Tr11	Tr12	Tr13
Monday	2	9	16	23	30
Tuesday	3	10	17	24	31
Wednesday	4	11	18	25	
Thursday	5	12	19	26	
Friday	6	13	20	27	
Saturday	7	14	21	28	

September 2021

Sunday		Tr14	Tr15	Tr16	Tr17
Monday		6	13	20	27
Tuesday		7	14	21	28
Wednesday	1	8	15	22	29
Thursday	2	9	16	23	30
Friday	3	10	17	24	
Saturday	4	11	18	25	

October 2021

Sunday		Tr17	Tr18	Tr19	LstTr	4bAdv
Monday		4	11	18	25	
Tuesday		5	12	19	26	
Wednesday		6	13	20	27	
Thursday		7	14	21	28	
Friday	1	8	15	22	29	
Saturday	2	9	16	23	30	

November 2021

Sunday		3bAdv	2bAdv	ChrK	Adv1
Monday	AllSs	8	15	22	29
Tuesday	2	9	16	23	30
Wednesday	3	10	17	24	
Thursday	4	11	18	25	
Friday	5	12	19	26	
Saturday	6	13	20	27	

December 2021

Sunday		Adv2	Adv3	Adv4	Chr1
Monday		6	13	20	27
Tuesday		7	14	21	28
Wednesday	1	8	15	22	29
Thursday	2	9	16	23	30
Friday	3	10	17	24	31
Saturday	4	11	18	Chr	

On Sunday 27 December 2020 John, Apostle and Evangelist may be celebrated.

On Sunday 3 January The Epiphany may be celebrated, transferred from 6 January.

On Sunday 31 January The Presentation of Christ may be celebrated, transferred from 2 February.

On Sunday 31 October All Saints' Day may be celebrated, transferred from 1 November.